Dutch

Preacher

Boy

Dutch Preacher Boy

Coming of Age in Grand Rapids,

Taking Wing Beyond*

TUNA FISCH

*From Ethnocentric Religion to a Wide World of Wonder

A MEMOIR

2021

Dutch Preacher Boy

Copyright © 2021 by John Kommerinus Tuinstra
TunaFisch Publishing
www.tunafisch.com

Library of Congress Cataloging-in-Publication Data

Print ISBN: 978-1-09838-2-513
eBook ISBN: 978-1-09838-2-520

FOR

My Wife and Family,
Rudy and Classmates,
Colleagues and Friends,
All Fellow Travelers

We shall not cease from exploration,
And the end of all our exploring
Will be to arrive where we started,
And know the place for the first time.

T.S. Eliot, "*Little Gidding*"

That old environment of childhood never goes away.
It doesn't matter how far or fast you run,
You don't outrun your childhood.

Paul Schrader, in *Thin Ice*

We tell ourselves stories in order to live.

Joan Didion, *The White Album*

Look at us, we are still alive!

Julia Scheeres, *Jesus Land*

To the world you may be one person;
But to one person you may be the world.

Dr. Seuss

TABLE OF CONTENTS

Los Angeles *1982—* *139*

CHAPTER ONE.

FAST FORWARD

Extraordinary! An angel of God startles me awake. *"Get up! They need you!"*

I, a seminarian on his first summer assignment, in Vermillion, South Dakota, am about to embark on an adventure of a lifetime.

It isn't a typical Sunday where I'd tackle heady issues from the Danforth Chapel pulpit, University of South Dakota campus. On this thirtieth day of July 1967, I had been invited to speak in rural Platte, a 130 mile, 2½ hour drive west.

Last night, with a rousing message ready to go, Platte calls: "We just had two deaths in our congregation, a middle aged woman and a young man. Please bring comfort." I scramble to reread, rethink, rewrite. Weariness sets in. Soon I am fast asleep at my desk.

Then, as if jarred by lightning, my eyes seize on the wall clock: *"7:45"*. Church starts at 9:30. I have exactly 1 hour, 45 minutes. What do I do? Call and cancel? *Not on your life.*

I jump into my three-piece suit, grab my Bible and notes, dash to the car, hit the highway, and am suddenly overwhelmed by a stunning double rainbow extending horizon to horizon - *a miracle, a sign. God is with me.*

In a flash of revelation, I visualize a private plane propelling me to my destination. There must be recreational pilots at the Vermillion airport.

No luck! *Think! Yes!* There's another airport at Yankton, thirty miles north, along the Missouri River.

I leap from my vehicle, spot a bystander near the runway. "You know of anybody coming in?"

"Sure do," he volunteers, "There's a single engine Piper from Nebraska about to land in three minutes." *My destined chariot in the sky!* I tell him what I need. "Well, it doesn't hurt to flag him down and ask," he deadpans.

The Piper lands and taxies. I sprint to the aircraft waving my arms frantically.

The pilot hops down, "What's the matter?"

"Listen, I'm late for church; I overslept. They need me desperately. Just get me to the church on time. I'll never make it by car.... How much? – to fly me to Platte?"

He hesitates slightly, then grins, "For you, preacher, forty bucks."

"Sold! Let's roll." (I have exactly $41.48 in my billfold). Who could possibly ask for more? Guardian angel, wondrous sign in the sky, calm weather, smooth ride, gorgeous view....

The little town of Platte comes into view. "Where's the airport?" I query.

"There isn't any. Just the grass strip over there. See the wind bag in that farmer's field?"

"No taxi service? How do I get to church?"

"Sorry, my friend. That one you'll have to figure out for yourself. Now hang on, it's gonna be a little bumpy...." He exits the scene with a modest military salute, "Good luck!" Under his breath, he mumbles, *"Angel, rainbow, church...hogwash!"* as he revs up the engine and takes to the air.

It's 9:20. Now I have to fend for myself. I spy the edge of town from the middle of this hot, humid, mosquito-infested field. I navigate the tall grass, elbow my way through corn stalks, hurdle two fences, jog past chicken coups and a pig pen. And as I approach a farmhouse, witnessing a car leaving the driveway, I shout at the top of my lungs, arms flailing – all to no avail!

In desperation, I pound on the front door of the house. No response. Time's running out. "*Lord, help!*" And from the corner of my eye – would you believe? – I spot a little kid's bike on the side lawn. "Forgive me, *mea culpa*, but I've got to steal – no, borrow - this bike, for the greater good."

So, off to the races, my knees hitting the handle bars, sweating profusely in my suit and tie.... Wait, this is how *The Platte Enterprise* (August 3, 1967) describes it (republished in *The Banner* as *"A Moral for Seminarians"*):

> "(John), student at Calvin Seminary (Grand Rapids, Michigan), probably won't soon forget his trip to Platte.... Junior DeLange, who lives near the airport, was just leaving for church, but failed to hear the distant shouts for a ride.
>
> The student, running slightly behind in his race with the clock, borrowed a bicycle (junior size) from DeLange's yard and peddled furiously. He began to breathe easier upon seeing First Reformed Church on the north edge of town, but then noticed it wasn't the right church. He peddled on.
>
> As he went down Main Street past Bob's Café, Marv Rasmussen was walking down the sidewalk. (John) asked where the Christian Reformed Church was located and quickly disappeared around the corner without pausing as Marv pointed west.
>
> You can imagine that Marv was somewhat puzzled. Here's a man in a dark suit, perspiration dripping from his face, a Bible under his arm, riding a half-size bicycle, as fast as he could go, who barely had time to wave his thanks as he zipped around the corner headed for the church...."[1]

It's 9:40. I lean the bike against a wall. An elder is busy leading the congregation in an improvised hymn sing, praying that the neophyte would

---

1   *The Platte Enterprise*, August 3, 1967. Permission granted by Sharon Huizenga, Publisher.

soon appear. I open the back door, hoping to find a bathroom and freshen up a little. But lo and behold - I find myself standing on the podium in full view of the congregation. What an entrance!

Mouths are agape. Before them stands a sweaty, disheveled greenhorn seminarian. The elder looks greatly relieved. Not missing a beat, I intone "Let us pray" (no explanations, no excuses). I breathe deeply, hold my urine, and somehow find the right words to say, words of comfort, words of hope - entirely off script.

Doxology completed, I scamper to the bathroom, and return to shake hands with the congregation. At this point, no one is yet wise to what happened, when all of a sudden a little boy shouts to his mother in earshot of everyone, "Mom, what's my bike doing over here!" That really got things buzzing.

I had to fess up, and told them the entire story. "And that, young man, is how your bike ended up against the wall of the church." Amazing how the *gravitas* of that morning turns at once into a *lightness of being*. The boy's parents come up to me, "You poor soul, you missed us by just seconds!"

A little later, Junior DeLange playfully taps me on the shoulder, "By the way, Pastor John, somebody was home - my elderly mother. But she was too frightened to open the door to that wild stranger. And guess what? There's one thing you probably missed - our garage door was unlocked; there's a Jeep inside, with keys in the ignition."

Whoa! After composing myself, I respond, "The Lord works in mysterious ways, but never would I take your Jeep!"

That day in Platte, we had a good cry. Afterward, we had a good laugh. Tragedy and comedy - such is life.

At summer's end, the new school year commenced - at a wooded retreat, as was customary. The tale was told of the ill-fated but miraculously-sustained tenderfoot, a tale passed on for many years - with a lesson for seminarians in two easy steps (*"Sleeper, awake!"* and *"Never give up"*), interspersed with hearty laughter. I was properly roasted. This would be a tough one to live down!

CHAPTER TWO.

PINNACLE OF POWER

Weeks after that hilarious escapade, a little tranquility was in order, but that was not to be. As the memory of my exotic rainbow begins fading, Thor's mighty thunderbolts rifle through the sky and rip through every atom of our cabin at the pinnacle of a bluff overlooking the vast Missouri. My fellow pastors dive for cover under their primitive bunks. I remain glued to the window.

"John, get away from there. You'll get killed!"

"Are you kidding? I wouldn't miss this for the world, come what may.... God's talking."

"Yes, he's telling you to get over here."

I forget the theme of that conference. Something like: "Why Can't Everybody Be Just Like Us?" But I couldn't get enough of this sight-and-sound extravaganza, unparalleled in human history, apart from Noah's Flood and the primeval chaos – louder even than Dmitri Shostakovich's Symphony #11, wilder than a myriad of big screen apocalyptic sagas.

My imagination flashes back to the year 1804 – Lewis and Clark desperately paddling toward a riverbank upstream, seeking shelter, their bodies soaked, their blistered hands tugging the oars with fury. And as these images flitter through my consciousness, a 'flying flame', a shaft of light, a bolt, a massive blinding missile, so enormous, awesome and dazzling, with a din so deafening, explodes - slamming into soft soil ten yards from the tip of my nose.

"*Ho-ly Mo-ly,*" I gasp; "*Hallelujah,*" I scream. As our shelter rattles, my body trembles. Such raw power – nerve-shattering, bone-chilling. Enough to transform sinner Saul into righteous Paul.

My dorm-mates are in shock: "The signs of the times", "The end is near", "Prepare to meet your maker". Happily, when the shivers and panic subside, we lay bare our feelings, voice our fears, and burst into giddy cathartic laughter.

In the encounter, we shovel for meaning as well. "Any lesson we can learn from this?" Answers flow freely: "Man, thou art mortal!" "Remember who's in charge here." "Humble yourself." "You've been spared for such a time as this." (A skeptical bystander might say, "We're just plain screwed.")

However, one voice emerges with unusual candor: "Well, this I know: when it's my time to go, I don't want a long, heroic battle with cancer, like my sister, father and best friend. *Let it be a merciful bolt of lightning.*"

Amen.

INTERLUDE

Upon immigrating from The Netherlands to Grand Rapids, Michigan in 1950, my first-grade classmates snicker, "Look what came up out of the ocean – *Tuna fish!*" It was, of course, a play on my name. "We'll call you Tuna"; and it stuck.

But why's a fish out of water, like me, writing a memoir? Because after fifty-some years of swimming with and against the tide, an email in 2015 surprises me. It's from Rudy, former classmate (grades one through twelve) and retired Grand Rapids Police detective, with three decades of dedicated service.

Rudy asks, "Where have you been all my life? We've drifted apart! Time to catch up."

"You mean, like two old codgers on a virtual park bench?"

"You got it! Where do we start?"

"Okay, remember sixth grade, Mayfield Christian? As the year progressed, our perfectly-coiffed, elegantly-dressed teacher acquired the nickname '*Hurricane Trudy*' (after the tempest then convulsing the Gulf of Mexico). She was a remarkably gifted chalk artist – but had a penchant for turning her chalk into chalk-missiles (tools of peace into instruments of war)! In her demand for perfection from others, and total control for herself, she exploded into sudden fits of classroom terrorism. *Dead aim!* What an eye! What a sting! Her muscle-flexing power placed us on constant alert. Had she been scouted by the Detroit Tigers, they would have forthwith drafted her into the minors. Well, not all was lost. We learned to duck and dodge like Rocky Marciano and butterfly Cassius Clay. I only marvel we never took action, returning fire!"

So begins five years of correspondence between friends in Grand Rapids and Los Angeles. After a couple of years, Rudy writes, "These are great memories. You've got to publish them before they're lost!" I hesitate; but Rudy's insistence carries the day.

We all have a story to tell. Even ordinary lives, like mine, have their extraordinary moments. *(I always wondered why I had so many of them!)* In this book, I offer for your enjoyment a few of these moments.

We make numerous critical choices on our journey, but there's always the *'Forrest Gump* factor' – that teasingly unpredictable *thrownness* into life. You never know whom you'll meet, what'll happen, or how it'll all turn out.

There's an advantage to sitting on our bench. We discover a pattern our minds impose on the randomness of the past.

But if the story is worth telling, it's got to be real, and it's got to be fun.

My story is that of a boy whose young life leads him to religious studies and leadership in the church, but who also discovers that life *outside the fold* holds an equally great attraction. He feels the centrifugal force of destiny tugging him beyond his ethno-religious roots and the city that nurtured him. Life can be incredibly unpredictable!

The action of the opening chapters takes place, chronologically, between chapters 19 and 20. More rip-roaring adventure can be found in chapters 24, 29 and 30. For a little eroticism, publicly articulated in seminary, chapter 23. Exciting competition: chapter 36. In-flight encounters with notable people: chapters 25, 26 and 49. There's something for everyone, including history, social commentary and serious reflection. Pick and choose.

Along the way: a peek inside Dutch aristocracy, Mexican border intrigue, threats in the jungle, sexual awakening, athletic fields of battle, heroes, tragedies, escapes, with lots of humor and playful banter. This is the story of one who discovers that the sacred is, in reality, secular - that 'the Kingdom' blazes a trail which is inescapably *of the earth earthy,* leading toward a truer and fuller humanity.

Two books encouraged me on this quest. First, the entertaining anthology *Thin Ice: Coming of Age in Grand Rapids* (2007). Second, the engrossing memoir *Jesus Land (2005),* by Julia Scheeres. A third influence: the perceptive writings of Joan Didion.

I do hope you, the reader, will tell your story. As you think about it, laugh and cry with me as I tell mine. And later, as I read yours, may laughter far outweigh the tears.

John Kommerinus Tuinstra

(Tuna Fisch)

December 2020

San Diego, California

THE NETHERLANDS

1943—1950

CHAPTER THREE.

WAR!

L et's begin at the beginning - my life before emigration to Grand Rapids. Fasten your seat belt and enjoy the ride!

With the aid of a midwife, in our little house in the town of Heerenveen, province of Friesland, The Netherlands, I emerged from the warm waters of my mother's womb November 1943 into a cold winter of war, the youngest of six siblings. Herr Hitler had hijacked Holland the tenth of May 1940.

The Huns invaded our land two days before Pentecost Sunday. The outpouring of the Spirit was brutally preempted by a swarming descent of paratroopers, aerial bombardment, tanks and heavy artillery. Queen Wilhelmina, the tough-tender matriarch of her people, fled to London with our national leaders, forming a government in exile. On *Radio Oranje,* via the British Broadcasting Company, she speaks like a modern-day Joan of Arc, instilling courage in the hearts of her oppressed, exploited subjects.

The BBC, spearheading a *"V" for Victory* campaign, opens its daily broadcasts with the powerful and heroic first four notes of Beethoven's Fifth Symphony, on tympani, which in Morse Code spells "V". It captures listener attention and fosters hope. Four notes become the musical insignia and unifying symbol of the entire Allied effort. Churchill characteristically raises his right hand and flashes a "V" with his index and middle fingers. Others follow his playbook.

My dad, born 1901, no stranger to war and economic depression, is a vital player in the Resistance for five years. Only my mother knows of his involvement; no one else does, and no one else may, not his children, not his relatives. Any leak entails certain death. They meet in windmills, barns, fields and forests. Female couriers on bicycles keep communication lines between them open, coordinating their efforts. Coded messages are cleverly embedded in BBC programming to guide their activities.

Tragically, however, even to possess a radio is a capital offense. Being caught means summary execution in the street in front of your house, as a deterrent to others. My dad takes the risk, listening to broadcasts at night, decoding the messages. Then he hides the radio, again and again, in a place he is convinced young Nazi soldiers will never look. (Troops made regular unannounced inspections of people's homes). Where? Under the mattress of my crib! They don't mess with innocent infants. Many have infants of their own in Germany. So I'm proud to say I've done my part to help win the war against those Nazi scoundrels!

In the midst of turmoil, curfews and endless restrictions, my parents decide to transcend the ordinary, by hiring a coach drawn by jet-black Frisian horses. Yes, we're just common people, but this is Saint Nicholas Eve, the day of my baptism. As my mother tells it, a young soldier strides up alongside our coach, shouting *"Halt! Wo gehen sie? Wie heissen sie?"* and "What are you hiding?" He looks; he sees. I smile. Tears suddenly trickle down the face of this pistol-wielding warrior; he melts. I am baptized with his tears. His humanity reawakened, sensing his vulnerability, he places his weapon in its holster, and speaks with considerable emotion: "I just received news of the birth of my son, our first-born. If only I could hold him now." The gently falling rains from gray skies above cannot wash away the poignancy of this moment. I smile, he weeps, while unbeknown to me, my countrymen weep as occupiers smile.

My oldest brother, William (Bill), was born near the onset of the Great Depression in 1929, just weeks apart from Anne Frank and Audrey Hepburn. Each progressed from age 10 through 15 during the war. Anne's

Diary remains an inspiration to us all. Audrey's anguish and ecstasy is vividly narrated in *Dutch Girl: Audrey Hepburn in World War II* (2019) – an incredible story of survival and selfless service in heavily besieged Arnhem (subject of the film *A Bridge Too Far,* 1977). My brother insists it wasn't all misery: 'Sure, no denying it was a world of food and fuel shortages, ration coupons, schools turned into enemy headquarters and military hospitals, aerial dogfights, refugees streaming up from the south, neighbors disappearing without a trace…. But we're kids; we consider ourselves invincible; and we're determined to do the things we love.

'Near Wars end, Hitler's henchmen cut off electricity to several pumping stations. As a consequence, the below-sea-level farmland surrounding our town, ordinarily protected by dikes, is flooded. By this means, the Germans create a defensive perimeter for themselves against Allied invasion. Bad for farmers, but a bonanza for boys with skates – a winter paradise in the midst of hell.' Skating is Bill's passion. There are miles and miles of hard, smooth ice on which to race and sail. Yes, sail! 'We unbutton our jackets, spread our arms out wide, and let the heavy winds propel us. We attach steel runners to wooden crates, and use old curtains or bed sheets as sails connected to a pole. A potent gust of wind hurtles us forward at breakneck speed. We're free! We're truly free!'

For months, squadrons of Allied bombers drone on overhead from England to targets in Germany. Some are met with anti-aircraft fire amid skirmishes of fighter planes. When hit, my brother reflects, 'We'd see little white specks in the sky, gradually coming into focus as parachutes. Many airmen are rescued and hidden by the Underground. One night, fast asleep, I dream I am flying in one of those bombers that was struck. I have no choice but to bail out. My parachute is secure. I'm heading toward the exit door; I'm about to turn the handle – when, suddenly, I hear my dad shout, *"Jongen!* (Boy), what are you doing!" He grabs me and pulls me back just in the nick of time. I had been sleepwalking. I was in the process of opening my upstairs bedroom window, ready to jump out! This incident shook me up to such a degree that I never sleep-walked again (as far as I know!)'.

Two days after the death of Franklin Delano Roosevelt (of Dutch heritage, and dearly loved by our people), on April 14, 1945, Canadian troops sweep in from the east and south of our town, liberating the patriots of Heerenveen. There is dancing in the streets. However, my brother states, 'Our family's celebration is tempered by anxiety. Dad and his platoon are still fighting "Fritz" north of town. He's been absent two weeks, struggling to free farms and smaller populations. We fear the worst. What a relief when the next day we see a bicycle approaching. There he is, rifle slung over his shoulder. "He's alive!" - a true hero of the Resistance.'

Bill, age fifteen, keeps pressing our dad, "Did you kill anybody? Did you?" Dad refuses to talk about it. 'But one day, he felt the need to put my questions to rest, and said "Okay, but I'm only going to tell you once, and it will never be spoken of again. The last soldier I had to kill, in self-defense, turned out to be a boy, age fifteen, exactly your age." He spoke of this with deep emotion. When he saw the body, he was overwhelmed with grief. I listened, stored it away. He never mentioned it again. I never dared ask.

'Dad spoke of Nazi cruelty to captured Resistance fighters. He and his cohorts, by contrast, were resolved not to treat their own captives the same way. They saw no gain in retributive kills (although no one would have blamed them). They didn't line up the enemy and execute them, or hang them from local trees. Remarkably, their last act before heading home was an order to their captives: "Remove your belts; leave them right here." (All their belt buckles were stamped with the biblical messianic words *"Gott Mit Uns"* – sheer blasphemy in Calvinist eyes. In practical terms, it meant: Hitler is god; he is with us; he'll take care of us). "Now *Go!* Start walking. *That* way". And since they all wore baggy trousers, it was quite a sight to see them go on their way, trying to keep their pants up. They wouldn't get very far; they'd be met by Canadian troops.'

CHAPTER FOUR.

TICKET TO FREEDOM

Now that we've put the Hun on the run, allow me to indulge in a little family humor. I heard tell of my great grandfather Fonk, who lost a leg in an accident. To help him overcome the trauma of his loss, his wife insisted: What we need is a full burial ceremony for your leg. Following the solemn ritual, in which the preacher reminded them of the fragility of life and the imperative to make it count, the casket was lowered, dirt scooped over it, and a headstone put in place, with the epitaph (my translation from Frisian): "Here lies Fonk's leg, in this hollow; later, old man Fonk will follow". No more soccer for great grandpa.

As fate would have it, we lived right next door to the most illustrious international soccer star the Dutch ever produced, long before the advent of Johan Cruyff. (Compagnonstraat twelve; we were number ten). What are the odds? He was the Joe DiMaggio of his day. Today his statue graces the plaza of the stadium which bears his name: Abe Lenstra Stadion.

Abe (born 1920) and his brother Jan (born 1919) taught my older brothers (Bill, George, Ted) the tricks of the trade, before the war. Bill reminisces: 'Abe and Jan practice in the street in front of our house, attempting to set new records – keeping the ball in the air as long as possible, heading it to each other and solo-bobbing it vertically. They use us kids as practice posts, line us up in various ways, then dribble around us as fast as they can. They persist in kicking the ball against the side of our house, which drives mother crazy. Abe keeps experimenting with new moves, challenging us to take the ball from him. He heads the ball, rolls it over his shoulders, bounces it up with his knees or feet, then dribbles it down the street. We are dumbfounded, unable to defend. Like a magician, he angles the ball into a gutter, making it disappear. We never notice. Thinking he still has the ball, we chase him – until he stops, points to the ball behind us, and cracks up laughing. So do we!

'All league games are played Sunday afternoon, but we have to go to church. As soon as we hear the final "Amen", we dash to a friend's house next to the stadium, climb his tree in our Sunday best, and watch the last half hour of the game. When Abe scores, we roar. We witness the fruit of all those tireless workouts in the street. He becomes famous for feigning moves, utterly confusing players of the opposition.

'I remember old man Lenstra: short, stocky, loud, boisterous. If Jan and Abe lost their match, it would incur his wrath. He would spew out the choicest cuss words ever invented in the Frisian language. They echoed through the neighborhood, leaving no doubt as to who won and who lost!'

Abe's mother was petrified one day when she noticed my daredevil brother Ted doing handstands on our chimney. 'Theo (Ted), get down from there! You're not in the circus. Play ball, not Russian roulette!' And so he did, dribbling his soccer ball wherever he went – until, one day in 1944 (age ten), he kicks it over a wall at Nazi precinct headquarters down the street. Impulsively, he scales the wall, scrambles toward the ball, but before you can yell "Go-o-o-al", a powerful hand grabs him by the neck and drags him into their war room. From there, solitary confinement in a bathroom – enough to scare the wits out of any free spirit.

He does exactly as his older brothers advised: 'If you're ever caught, scream at the top of your lungs: *Ich habe nichts getan! Ich habe nichts getan!* ("I didn't do anything!"). He shouts all right, and then belts out every song he ever learned at school over and over again – which, after several hours, annoys his captors so much, they hurl him into the street with a swift kick he'd never forget.'

Later, this singing captive would become a tenor in the Dallas Opera. This acrobat and scaler of walls would be seen doing showy swan dives off the tower platform at Soft Water Lake (Grand Rapids). And this passionate ball dribbler would come to be the first captain and goalie of a Dutch squad (mostly Canadian) which morphed into the Calvin College Men's Soccer Team.

As for me, the late 1940s were a ceaseless adventure. No sooner does a Dutch boy learn to walk, and he finds his feet shod with skates, pushing a kitchen chair over frozen canals. Next comes a bicycle, my ticket to freedom. Not to worry – everybody watches out for everybody in this town, where nothing goes ungossiped.

I know which relatives maintain the best inventory of candy, cookies and chocolate. So, I ring their doorbell. "Ach, Jan-a-man (little John), come in, come in."

"Thank you kindly," I chirp. After being seated and offered tea, I never fail to say: "My mother told me it's impolite to ask for cookies or chocolate. So, as you can see, I'm not doing that!" Having planted the seed, however, harvest was destined to follow. And upon taking my leave, I entreat them, "If my mother wonders, please let her know I never asked!" I think I was the best fed kid in town.

CHAPTER FIVE.

PARADISE

I spent a portion of my youth in an enchanted paradise. It was the fairy-tale weekend estate of an aristocratic Amsterdammer. *Vijverhof* lay just south of *Soestdijk Palace*, and a stone's throw from *Drakensteyn Castle (Lage Vuursche)*, residence of Prince Bernhard and Princess Juliana.

Let me explain. It's all about my uncle and aunt, Jan and Kommerina, with whose names I was baptized (the feminine *-a* was altered to masculine *-us*). They had no children, and as such became indulgent second-parents to me. Luck of the draw!

Oom Jan was loving, loads of fun, gregarious, intelligent. As extra income, he chauffeured the above-mentioned affluent gentleman. One day, in Amsterdam, a bicycle bolted from around a corner in front of his vehicle. The boy he struck died shortly thereafter.

My uncle was inconsolable. But his client had a solution: 'Jan, I want you to become butler and overseer of my country estate, away from this city. There you can heal, and be at peace.'

Several times a year my dad commandeers his company's black Ford, and together with my mother, transports me to the magical abode of my second-parents. I am treated like royalty, and take full advantage of it! The owner, G. H. Crone (1884-1961), President of the Amsterdam Chamber of Commerce, was the grandson of a prominent colonialist, whose Indonesian plantations and Dutch import company, established in 1790, made him wealthy. The grandfather's portrait hangs in the Rijksmuseum near several Rembrandts.

My father's father was himself wedged into this colonial system. Born in 1868, and raised in a Dickens-like public orphanage (think *Oliver*, 1968), the Dutch army recruited him to help protect commercial interests on the islands – the mines and plantations (1885-1895). (Check out the film *Max Havelaar*, 1976). He was, during those years, a non-religious hell-raiser, a wild child with an overblown ego. I have little doubt he sired a significant number of interracial children. Just think – thousands of blood relatives in Indonesia! But I digress.

The Dutch had few natural resources, so they depended on import-export. They became the world's preeminent middlemen. For centuries it was said that a Dutchman was the only one who could buy from a Jew, sell to a Scot, and still come out with a profit! Today, this is ethnic stereotyping, but that was then.

I have the run of the estate, as do dozens of roaming peacocks. The smell of Douglas Fir is intoxicating. Trails through the woods seem endless. Estate caretakers, all of whom become my friends, are instructed to keep an eye on me while they tend the gardens, greenhouse, orchard, stable, and miniature zoo, with its exotic birds and creatures.

One day, reminiscent of *Downton Abbey* (2010-2015), (with "Downstairs" forever obsessed with "Upstairs"), and of *Sabrina* (1995), my uncle motions to me: "Jan-a-man. *Sh-Sh!* Look through the crack of the door. There's Prince Bernhard!" The Prince, fighter pilot, war hero, leader of the Dutch Resistance and international businessman, was a close friend of Crone. Both were collectors – of almost everything under the sun, but especially choice animals, birds, postage stamps and ancient coins (Greek, Roman and Byzantine). That night, they bare their stamp collections for close scrutiny.

Juliana went on to become Queen in 1948. The Dutch lost their Indonesian holdings in 1949. And the Prince founded the Bilderberg Group, which to this day sponsors an annual closed-door conference of the world's top political and corporate leaders to foster free market capitalism.

Sadly, womanizing, and bribe-taking from Lockheed, Northrup and other giant corporations ruined this hero's personal reputation. How the mighty are fallen!

I was absent the day a chauffeur rang the bell at the front gate of the estate. Flat tire. The master of the house, in an exceptionally contrary mood, issues a directive: 'Send him away; can't help him'. My uncle slips out and aids him nonetheless. Mission accomplished, a back window rolls down, and two ladies express their gratitude – would you believe: Princess Beatrix, along with Queen Juliana's confidante, Greet Hofmans. I don't know if Bernhard's good friend ever learned whom he turned away, but one thing is certain, Oom Jan was like the Parson in Chaucer's *Canterbury Tales*: "First he wrought, and afterward he taught."

My uncle taught me early on: Don't be fooled or intimidated by people with aristocratic airs, by prelates, popes, politicians or potentates. They're all just human; they're fallible. Hold your head up high; we're of equal worth and dignity; and we're here to do good. My mother was quick to add: Let responsible women take the lead, and this will be a better world by far.

The presence of Greet Hofmans at *Soestdijk Palace* caused considerable commotion when Juliana asked her to use her faith-healing wizardry to cure Princess Marijke's deteriorating eye condition. Modern medicine prevailed, however, and in thankfulness for this humanly-mediated divine providence, Marijke's name was changed to Christina. Greet, unfortunately, stayed on at the Palace for years, as personal advisor to the Queen. Foolish? Indeed. "The Greet Hofmans Affair" exploded into a national crisis, as she kept pushing a pacifist agenda during the Cold War. The Prime Minister finally forced Juliana's hand, and Hofmans was removed from the Palace.

In 1961, the same year Bernhard created the World Wildlife Fund, Mr. Crone's Canadian-born widow (surname Black) willed *Vijverhof* to the Dutch people as a Nature Preserve (much like Huntington Gardens in San Marino, California), for the enjoyment of all, forever after to be called *Cronebos*. What I, as a child, imagined to be my private domain became the legacy of a new generation. Open wide the gates!

GRAND RAPIDS, MICHIGAN

1950–1969

CHAPTER SIX.

NEW WORLD

My pilgrimages to *Vijverhof* are soon to be eclipsed by a journey to the New World. Grand Rapids: "God's country," they say, "Jerusalem" – as theocratic as Salt Lake City. (Both also led the nation in domestic violence and divorce!) I fell in love with these hallowed precincts by the rapids – greatest place on earth for a kid with a bike to grow up.

But first: "We're going to America!" Our neighbors, friends and relatives are shocked. "It's for the kids," my parents explain, "for their future."

So at school, April 1950, classmates lead me through a gentle spanking machine, allowing them to express symbolic displeasure at my departure. From there they lift me onto a table, place a paper crown on my head, sing for me and present me with a lovingly crafted booklet of memories, asking me never to forget them. I haven't forgotten. It was a ritual of death and resurrection – the oldest theme in the religions and mythologies of mankind. We hug, then part. It feels like losing a close friend.

Next morning, our family of eight begins walking with fixed purpose to the train station. Having left my wooden shoes behind, I'm wearing my spit-polish shiny Sunday leathers. Then to my astonishment, our walk spontaneously transitions into a parade. Neighbors are at their windows, front doors and sidewalks waving and wishing us well. I love parades! The first person I wave to is an elderly neighbor, true royalist, who used to take pleasure in cursing the enemy occupation forces as *rot moffen* (freely translated, "dirty rotten fascists"), and belted out the *Wilhelmus* (national anthem) on Liberation Day, and thereafter, with abandon.

Passing through the bombed-out heart of Rotterdam, we board Holland America's *Nieuw Amsterdam*, third class. My oldest brother recalls: 'Jan-a-man, 6 ½ years of age, whom we older siblings had the task of watching, always managed to elude us, and when we did find him, was almost always somewhere in first class entertaining passengers and crew with his questions, while feasting on ice cream and French pastries!'

Speaking to me in Dutch, the aunt with whom we lodge in Grand Rapids presents me with a challenge the morning after we arrive. "Jan (John), how would you like to be the first one in your family to earn money in America?" She has my attention. "I'll tell you what – I'll give you your cousin's left-over morning newspapers *(Grand Rapids Herald)* every day. Take his five extras under your arm, knock on doors, and say "Want to buy a paper? Five cents." The only English I know is "Hello", "Goodbye" and "Coca Cola". With high hopes, and some trepidation, I go door to door, knock and ask: *"Vant to by a papr? Fijf sense."* I can't believe it; they sell like hotcakes! Nobody says "No". First day: twenty-five cents – a fortune. So every day, I make the rounds, just before the afternoon *Grand Rapids Press* is delivered. Most curious - the same people keep buying. They already have afternoon subscriptions, but bless their hearts, they see the bigger picture. The immigrants of blue collar southwest Grand Rapids remember what it is like to make a new beginning.

My parents purchase 1111 Baldwin Street SE for $10,000 – a decent neighborhood in those days, within walking distance of everything we need: church, school, stores, and especially the Fulton Street Farmers Market. I immediately enter into a verbal contract with several Dutch-speaking shut-in elderly neighbors to pick up and deliver fresh fruit and veggies, along with groceries from Bomgaars, adjacent to the Market. Bomgaars is old-world, like "Little House on the Prairie" – no self-service. Give him the list; he fetches; and: *Ka-ching!* Very simple. The ladies give me a dime for each run, and these dimes multiply swiftly.

The Community store down the street is, by contrast, a forerunner of 'super' stores like Meijer's. Democratization. Help yourself, then pay at the checkout. Who would have thought! The proprietor always greets his clients with the words *"Are you sad, mad or glad?"* Good psychology; it never fails to elicit a smile and spark a conversation – even if you'd heard it for the thousandth time.

The schoolyard, however, is something else. I feel like a fish out of water. I desperately want to belong. Will I be accepted? The mockery begins (I suppose, to test my mettle) with the old saw: *"Dutchman, Dutchman, belly fulla' straw, can't say nothin' but ya(w), ya(w), ya(w)!"* As big Freddy begins shoving and punching me, Billy comes to my rescue, pulls me aside, and reveals some key information: "He's a bleeder," punctuating his remark with a bold gesture, "just punch him in the nose!" Sure enough, he bleeds profusely – after which we are friends, not adversaries. That is the decisive moment, the breakthrough. And having won that coveted acceptance, they name me *Tuna fish.*

But the frustration of being English-illiterate leads me to act out in class. I've lost count of how many visits I've been compelled to make to the principal's office. He literally puts me over his knee and applies a wooden bottom whacker. I guess corporal punishment is still the norm in this new nation. With every encounter he looks more menacing, applies more oomph and paddles me crimson! Christian school! Later, I learned he himself was acting out of frustration - scapegoating. He had a son languishing in State Prison.

With elementary mastery of English, and a new bicycle, comes freedom. Nothing more exhilarating! My bike is my earthly salvation. Now I can satisfy my insatiable curiosity by asking questions in English, spread my wings and explore this illustrious city. It isn't enough just to watch *"Sky*

King" and "*The Lone Ranger*" on a neighbor's brand-new, small-oval-screen black-and-white TV set (one of the first in town). I peddle to WOOD-TV (formerly WLAV-TV) and ask to be shown around. They are pleased to do so; I never doubted they would. Next, the fire department, police station, public library, YMCA (where, I discover, boys and men are required to swim nude. *Hygiene, they say; perverts, I muse*), Fanatorium (where I watch national bowling champion Marion Ladewig practice), and the *Grand Rapids Press*.

Fascinating. I simply introduce myself: "I'm new in town. I'd like to know how things work here. Could you show me around and tell me what you do?" Never fails. The guys at the very top turn out to be the most down to earth. They perhaps find it amusing. I find it illuminating. And they aren't even Dutch Christian Reformed. How cool is that! I begin feeling part of a larger whole, which is worth embracing. Ecumenical. These are people I like and trust.

But there is also church - Dennis Avenue Christian Reformed Church. I help the janitor straighten out after services – all for the thrill of stepping up behind the pulpit, gesturing wildly, projecting my voice to the back rafters and marveling at the reverberations. (The basic rules are: Stand up, so they can see you. Speak out, so they can hear you. Sit down, so they will like you.) "*No greater calling*", *they claim;* "you've gotta be a preacher". Maybe so, but the world's a big place.

I ask about the mansion on the backside of Hermitage Street. "Oh, a monastery, a religious order. They're Sodomites." I had heard of Franciscans and Dominicans, but never Sodomites. I store this in my memory for another day.

CHAPTER SEVEN.

SHAME

Klaas was a strange man. Visiting with my friend Rudy's parents Sunday nights after church, he became impulsively restless and impatient to leave. He'd rush to his car, race the engine, lay on the horn, and shout until his wife finally exited. Neighbors, needless to say, were perturbed. Rudy's family was embarrassed.

But that wasn't all. One day, in his 'professional' capacity, he took a garden hose and drenched their living room walls. Quickest way to strip wallpaper, he insisted, as water dribbled through the floorboards into the basement.

He was indeed one of a kind. At age fifteen, summer of 1959, I worked as his 'apprentice painter' for seventy-five cents per hour. During breaks, we'd feast on his superb home-made pastries and breads. For me it actually became a pastoral listening-apprenticeship. I learned that as a baker in the old country, a hostile partner did him in. Klaas never forgave him. He took that pain, anger and resentment with him across the ocean. It never let him go, because he never let it go – forever running the same old tape in his mind. It was like PTSD. Today, thank goodness, there is clinical help. Yet, for all that bombast and bluster, he was a man you could forever count on as champion of the down-and-out, the first to help in time of need.

These images summon related memories. His youngest daughter, a few years older than me, was absolutely gorgeous – every adolescent's wet dream. But then, there was his son, ten years my senior, who in the early 1950s invited me into his room. "John, have some sweets. Take your pick…. Come here, sit next to me." Slowly but surely, I feel him all over me, fondling my prepubescent self. I'm numb; I feel trapped. Afterward, he gives me a silver-coated ring in the shape of a saddle, which fits perfectly. *Consider the symbolism!* "John, I like you very much; I want you to be my special friend." *If I were older, that would have been a cue to run as fast as possible, as in "Run, Forrest, Run!"*

It became apparent he loved to ride a soft saddle. He was a pedophile. The silver ring functioned in his devious mind as hush money, with the prospect of future docility and compliance. After all, who can say no to a 'friend' who singles you out as 'special' with an alluring gift? One of the oldest tricks in the book! His was a perverse interpretation of "Let the children come unto me" (and he wasn't even a priest). I keep quiet; I am ashamed.

Shortly thereafter, my mother is hospitalized and I am farmed out to other friends of the family for six days, assigned to share a bed with one of their sons, five years older than me. He's big in every respect, fully grown. For him, I'm an easy target, and he takes full advantage. Five full nights I am his Venus (or Adonis) dropped from heaven. He tells me this is all perfectly normal – a transition from childhood to adulthood – a sort of initiation, or sticky baptism. I know there's nothing normal about this. It's more than just a slimy mess; it's subtle and overt coercion, rape - not free consent. I say nothing; I am ashamed.

When frustrated, I act out. Since my bicycle and I have the run of Grand Rapids, not long after the events I just described, I return to a place I like, the Grand Rapids Art Institute on Fulton Street. I spot their most valuable acquisition at the time, the centerpiece of their collection, a late Middle Age Madonna-and-Child. I remember vividly the first thrust I make with my Boy Scout jackknife – *directly into the penis of the Christ Child!* Unfortunately, two other classmates are with me that day. They follow my lead and damage other paintings. We are caught, and remanded into the custody of our parents. *I am shocked at my own actions; I'm not one to destroy!* Our parents had to come up with funds to pay for restoration. The incident hit the news cycle. We had to live with our shame that year in fourth grade, and then find ways of moving beyond it.

Everyone assumed the incident was an act of youthful indiscretion. No doubt it was. I didn't fully understand my motivation at the time. Not until years later did the cause and effect become clear to me as I spoke of this with a trusted friend. In fact, talking about it was liberating. I desired no contact with the molesters. Vengeance was not in my vocabulary. In both early Greek philosophy, as well as modern psychology, many have taught that it's not what happens to you that is the most important thing in life (stuff happens!), but how you respond. And *it's your response that shapes your character*, makes you what you are. You can choose to become bitter or better.

My mother (who knew nothing of the molestation – nobody did) was a great encourager, a natural positive thinker (never having read Norman Vincent Peale), and led me on the road called 'better'. That initial feeling of shame and anger, which erupted into acting out, followed by overt shaming and remorse, was a decisive turning point in my life. I had a strong will, and made a resolution to turn the manure into fuel for a better life.

CHAPTER EIGHT.

BIG SPLASH

Franklin Park pool, across from the old Calvin College campus, was most enticing to us 1950s kids on hot, muggy summer days. It was fully integrated – black kids, white kids. We thought nothing of this; this was the norm. Side by side we earned our "Junior Lifeguard Certificate" (I still have mine), and frolicked to our hearts content.

Reinder Van Til was also there, and describes better than anyone (in the anthology *Thin Ice*, 2007) the debut and ongoing antics of Buster Mathis (1943-1995), a big black gentle giant. We dared him "to do a cannonball off the high dive. ...For his payday of nickels and his moment of notoriety, Buster would spring high off the board, wrap his huge body into a ball, and hit the water like a runaway boulder plunging into a lake. The splash, as we hoped, would always shower cold water on the lifeguard sunning himself on his elevated perch, and this would inevitably lead to Buster's expulsion from the pool."[2] This is exactly what happened.

Buster Mathis, of course, became one of the great heavyweight boxers of the world, fighting the likes of Joe Frazier and Mohammed Ali. (His son, Buster Mathis Jr., followed in his father's footsteps). What Grand Rapidian Marian Ladewig was to bowling, Harold Worst to billiards, Gerald Ford and Rocky Rosema to football, Mickey Stanley to baseball, and Jack Lindhout to stock car racing, Buster was to boxing. He made a big splash.

---

2   Reinder Van Til, "Sins and Misdemeanors on the Southeast Side," in *Thin Ice* (Grand Rapids: Eerdmans, 2007), 220.

But it isn't just about big names. Every year, in the fifties, many of us would head to the Armory to participate in a BB gun competition. Great fun; nothing to lose; just give it your best shot. One outstanding competitor, who had won many ribbons, has no arms, just stubs – a thalidomide baby. He does everything with his legs and feet. Most remarkable! He lies on his back in the shape of a curved rocking chair runner, holds the rifle with his legs and pulls the trigger with his big toe. Bullseye! He needs no help; he wants no help, and certainly no pity. He is courageous and self-sufficient. And at the break, he eats his lunch with his feet. No complaining, just a positive attitude and lots of good humor. A no-name, but a true champion!

Churchy things also occupy our attention. Our isolationist denomination refuses to adopt Boy Scouts, and creates its very own "Calvinist Cadet Corps" in 1952. (In reality, it's a carbon copy of Boy Scouts). In those early years, I'm lucky to be chosen as a member of its Model Club, one of twelve cadets that travel out of state, showing others how to replicate our activities. Within a few years, over a thousand cadets gather at Camp Roger, by Little Bostwick Lake, for the first-ever Calvinist Cadet Corps Camporee. An ox is roasted on a huge spit over an open fire, which had to be tended for over twenty-four hours.

Just before carving and distributing the meat, Director Jake asks, "John, could you stand behind the mike (we had all formed a large circle around the ox – like a Canaanite religious ritual, or a mass of humanity encircling the *Kaaba* in Mecca) and pray for a blessing on this meal?" I almost did it in my pants! Thankfully, that did not happen.

I responded, "Sure thing." The circle ritual must have worked wonders, because that was the tenderest, juiciest, tastiest meat that ever passed our lips!

CHAPTER NINE.

MAKING THE CUT

As kids, one of our favorite haunts was Ramona Park, by Reeds Lake in East Grand Rapids. Not only was the wooded lake a splendid place to bike, but that double-track wooden roller coaster was for us the thrill of a lifetime!

A previous generation of Dutch Calvinists, however, considered Ramona Park the Devil's outhouse, rife with "worldliness" (booze, dancing, games of chance), the enemy of "godliness".

Sheri Venema (in the anthology *Thin Ice*, 2007)[3] tells of her immigrant grandparents, in 1911, whose newborn 2 ½ pound preemie twins had a zero chance of survival. No doctor or hospital could help. Without hope and wrenched with grief, the parents submitted to the inexorable will of divine providence.

Their oldest daughter burst into the living room with news: 'There's hope! Ramona Park. They have some invention called an "incubator". Inside, a tiny infant is struggling to stay alive. People are lining up and paying good money to see this child'.

'Ramona Park? In a pavilion, next to a freak show? People paying for a peek at our twin daughters? We can't do that!'

---

3   Sheri Venema, "Mux at Ramona," in *Thin Ice* (Grand Rapids: Eerdmans, 2007), 269-77. This is my thumbnail sketch of nine pages of narrative.

'But it's their only hope for survival!'

'No, it wouldn't be right!'

'Okay, then, talk to Reverend Breen.'

Dominee Evert Breen (Grandville Avenue Christian Reformed Church), sensitive to the stuff of moral ambiguity, lent his authoritative voice: 'God will be more pleased with the life of the twins than be threatened by the dregs of a circus.'

The preacher prevailed; the parents exclaimed: 'Let's do it – now!'

There they were – two precious preemies on public display. Large crowds came, for months, paying their ten cents admission. One twin died; the other lived.

So it was, in those days at least, that worldly amusements won out over Dutch Calvinist isolation.

The mention of Grandville Avenue reminds me of Dominee Breen's successor who in his retirement taught us catechism, while our church (Dennis Avenue CRC) had no pastor (1952-54). He was grandfatherly and told great stories. But stories were also told about him.

He and a worthy opponent, had been in dead-heat competition for the Chair of Old Testament at Calvin Seminary. The debate in Synod went on and on, and several rounds of voting ended in a tie. At last, the tie was broken, and he telephoned his wife (in Dutch): "*Lieve, 'tis mis. 'k heb het niet gewonnen. Hij is besneden, en ik niet.*" Loose paraphrase: My love, it was a toss-up. Someone passed the word that, since it's the Chair of Hebrew and Old Testament, the winner ought to be somebody that's circumcised. Turns out he is, and I'm not! Bummer. I didn't make the cut!

One more. There was a story going around, back in the day, about a CRC in northwest Grand Rapids that was experiencing a steep decline in numbers.

"So, what do we do?" they asked, "Pray? Knock on doors? Have more kids? Encourage immigration? Merge?" They were mostly older, one foot in the grave.

At a sparsely attended evening service, the struggling pastor was gripped by a celestial vision. He waxed eloquent and pronounced: "You all think we're dying, declining, disappearing? Well, I have news for you – it's not true. It's a lie – because when I look out at these vast numbers of pews, they're not empty, as it may seem. They're filled with the angels of heaven! (*Vibrato* in his voice) The angels are here; they're all around us. We're not alone. In this hallowed hall, the church militant and the church triumphant are one."

Amid this rousing rhetoric (one could almost hear celestial harps and choirs in the background), an old man jumped to his feet, the Dutch immigrant janitor, with broken English, no longer able to contain himself: "But dominee, we got a problem. Dem angels don't put no money in de collection plate!"

CHAPTER TEN.

ROCKY

Summer 1954

Who can forget our long hikes on country railroad tracks? (Think of *Stand By Me*, 1986). At the precipice of pubescence, eight of us take backpacks, canteens, lunches (peanut butter-jelly sandwiches), baseball caps and cards…and after a couple hours hiking, singing, joking, telling gross stories, we're starved and find a tranquil, grassy cove near the tracks.

During a burst of laughter, one of our troops jumps up, takes the lead and, for whatever reason, challenges the group to a contest, declaring: "Okay guys, drop your shorts and prove you're a man! First one to jack off wins." (What's he been smoking?)

Well, it must have been mass psychology; everybody was in. He gave the impression he himself had it worked out to a science. In his cocksureness he said things like "No, that's not how you do it; you do it like this…"!

Never in the history of mankind had so great an effort produced such little result.

Chalk it up to an interesting stage of life.

I forget who won.

April 3, 1956 is one of those days that for me will live in infamy. That evening, while at the roller rink in northeast Grand Rapids, gliding along to rhythms flowing from its mighty Wurlitzer, the lights flicker. The house goes black; the organ freezes; skaters slam into each other, hogpiling and screaming. Raw panic, confusion, chaos, pandemonium prevails!

Shortly thereafter, a powerful invisible force violently rips open the double doors at the north end – followed by the ominous roar of a freight train, as every panicking soul stumbles toward the exit.

We look out the door. A ferocious black tornado heads directly at us! We're about to be swallowed and spit out! Awesome, but terrifying. We stand there in mortal dread.

Miraculously, at the very last moment – literally! – the monster veers to the east, a split second away from almost certain annihilation. The malicious intruder spins its way south, then west, finally devastating a large swath of Hudsonville. It was a taste of the End.

Fall 1958: Our Christian school forbade tackle football. But so did our neighboring public Junior High. Their rationale? Apart from questions of liability, our maturing bodies are vulnerable to major injury. Further *Christian* rationale? Our bodies are "temples of the Holy Spirit". Yet, nothing can stop us. We are young and reckless, with visions of glory on athletic fields of battle.

Just up the hill from our campus is a vacant four-acre lot. Abandoned for years, overgrown with weeds, we seize the opportunity. We mow the weeds, chalk our perimeter and yard lines. "All they can do is throw us out." We each purchase a helmet and shoulder pads, and challenge our counterparts at the public school to six games. They agree, and we christen our lot "Star Field". We pool our paper route money and hire a referee. This is to be a serious rivalry, and – who knows? – perhaps the start of a new league.

We consider our team invincible – until Rocky Rosema walks onto the field, and our optimism quickly evaporates! Yes, the same Rocky that would star at Central High, the University of Michigan (in the footsteps of Gerald Ford) and the St. Louis Cardinals. This is where he got his start.

Rocky is big, strong, naturally athletic, runs circles around us, easily breaks through our lines – a formidable presence. It takes two or three of us to tackle him. Needless to say, our worthy opponents won all those games – except for one, when their champion was absent.

Rocky achieved glory and made his city proud. January 2020, he went on to glory in that other sense; he died - after suffering from dementia, brought on by multiple concussions. But before he slipped into that dark night of the mind, he asked his two daughters to promise they would never allow his grandsons to play football. They've held to that promise.

So, how about that old prohibition against tackle football? Perhaps it wasn't so stupid after all!

Today, that hallowed field which once cultivated a young star, has become a cultivated farm (Hillcrest Community Garden, Lyon Street NE), tackling the challenge of wholesome food for healthy brains and bodies.

CHAPTER ELEVEN.

HENRY

June 1952

I remember the day my trusty Schwinn rocketed me to the Grand Rapids Public Museum, Jefferson Avenue.

Incredible! Look at that enormous whale skeleton suspended from the ceiling. I feel like Jonah – as if this space were an ocean, and that creature is hungry. I escape to side rooms and discover lush life-like dioramas with native flora and fauna (deer, elk, bear); then other displays with all things terrestrial: animal, vegetable and mineral. (The celestial – a planetarium – is being planned). Darwin and evolution are implicit in all this – most exciting; so much to know!

I catch the eye of Miss Evelyn Grebel. "You look enthused," she remarks.

"I am. Never seen anything like this!"

"Well, why don't you join our summer program? Starts in a week."

"I'd love it. Is there any way I can help you?"

"First, John, learn all you can; then I may find ways you can help"

(I felt like young Lord Blakeney in *Master and Commander*, 2003).

Miss Grebel (Christian Science practitioner, opera buff and enthusiastic member of the Horatio Alger Society) had a positive influence on budding minds. Adhering to the philosophy of John Dewey, she drew out the best in kids, cultivating their leadership ability. She wanted children to mentor and lead others their own age.

Sure enough, school year 1952-53, she appoints me, age eight, Assistant Usher for the museum's Saturday morning movie matinees (nature films, cartoons, newsreels of the week) – two showings, six-hundred kids - before television begins its inexorable transformation of our lives. It requires no little effort to maintain tranquility and order in an auditorium suffused with youthful banter, especially when the 16mm projector has a mind of its own and causes untimely delays. Next two years: I'm Chief Usher; and my friend Henry becomes Assistant.

Henry was a natural with kids, fun, likable, empathetic, and generous. He bought ice cream for children, total strangers who didn't have a penny in their pocket, when he saw them gazing through the window of the soda fountain. But his generosity didn't end there. When offered a *Grand Rapids Press* route, he said, "Tuna, I'm sorry you didn't get it, so I'll tell you what – I'll split it with you fifty-fifty; we'll share the work and the profit, until you are awarded your own route." It is the gentrified neighborhood *Heritage Hill*, Fulton Street, surrounding the newly-constructed Central Reformed Church. Six months later I am given an adjacent route, and dub it 'my little gold mine'.

We are expected to collect payment from our customers once a week. I persuade most to do so once per month. Strange thing, people don't just pay; they talk. The route becomes a laboratory of sorts. I see human nature at its best, and at its worst. Of course, the only lab one needs is a family, a neighborhood, a school or a church; but a paper route provides even grander diversity. I can't believe the wide variety of beliefs, attitudes, interests, habits, addictions…. But one thing stands out: the poorest and humblest, widows and handicapped are the most appreciative, and tip beyond their means at Christmastime. A couple of the richest are revolting - ever complaining, slow to pay, manipulative, demanding, and no tip whatsoever!

We endure an extended strike at the *Grand Rapids Press* – the linotype typesetters union - and are asked to distribute 8 ½ x 11" news bulletins to our customers.

But that is nothing compared to the turmoil that ensues, at least for Sabbath-observing Christian Reformed paper boys like us. We, 'God's Elect', adamantly refuse to peddle the newly-introduced Sunday paper. The conflict in the air is as dense and vicious as an advancing thunderstorm (much like the Disney musical drama *Newsies*, 1992, in which paper boys go on strike against penny-pinching predatory publisher Joseph Pulitzer). Henry begs, "Tuna, I'm for peace and harmony; but you're also bold and outspoken. Do something!"

I storm the main office and ask for the chief. It takes a few visits, but finally the publisher opens his door, "Come in. Please have a seat.... John, I've heard your complaints and those of your religious compatriots. But we're in a modern era now. We don't want to go back to the old 'Blue Laws'." (I didn't know a Blue Law from blue cheese!) My response was something like Eric Liddell in *Chariots of Fire* (1981): "Keep the Sabbath Day holy"; and "He who honors me, I will honor".

What a relief that, after all this concerted pressure, a compromise took shape: 'Okay, Christian Reformed carriers, we are now giving you a choice: either have a sub deliver for you on Sunday mornings, or you can pick up your bundles directly from the printing plant Saturday afternoons and distribute them a day early'. Not bad! A fair solution. Kudos to the publisher.

All of our voices were heard, needs were addressed. And even though they rejected our rationale operative at that time (which even we ourselves abandoned at a later date), they found a way to stop the bleeding. They retained most of their readership as well as their young independent contractors.

I guess word got out back then about young Tuna's Sabbatarian militancy, so people from Rev. Henry Bast's church, Bethany Reformed (he was the radio preacher of *"Temple Time"*), decided to recruit this young firebrand to their cause. I said, "Right, how can I help?"

"There's an open meeting of the City Council we'd like you to attend with us. We need a young person to help us argue the evils of *pari-mutuel* betting – tomorrow night! We can't allow this corruption in our city; it's a slippery slope…. You'll be allotted about two minutes to make your case, so make it count.

"How?"

"Just tell them it'll be the ruination of future generations of young people like yourself. You don't have to know all the in's and out's. Trust us. Just sell the sizzle, not the steak. Your very youth will impress them."

So, in that crowded hall, I give my impassioned two minutes worth – but still have no idea what *"pari-mutuel* betting" is. Afterward, one of my brothers clues me in: "It's horse racing, dummy!"

"Oh, okay."

The Council ultimately decided it would not be good for the city.

CHAPTER TWELVE.

EASTER

Year 1958

My four oldest siblings have long since flown the family nest. Home consists of my parents, myself and an emotionally-mentally ill sister five years my senior. Her mood swings, growing up, were bad enough; now she has become increasingly uncontrollable. She drops out of eighth grade (isn't stupid, just disturbed) when her manic-depressive episodes multiply, and schizophrenia takes root. Her screams are interminable and unbearable, piercing my ear drums and my psyche. In open displays, she involuntarily tears off all her clothing, and bashes her head against the wall, struggling to expel her demons.

What's the cure? An exorcist? Drugs? Animal companionship? (She had walked away from her school and friends, and refuses to see a therapist). The war didn't help. As a child, she dove under the table, turned pale, shivered in fear, unable to choke back her tears, as fighter planes skirmished above, as bombs dropped and soldiers made headlong forays into our home.

The current chaos drives me crazy – ample reason to venture out and explore my surroundings. Henry is one of the few that can calm her and make her laugh. Old Klaas crafts an exquisite wooden cage for her pet monkey. Sadly, she quickly becomes bored with a long succession of pets, ever larger in size and more costly to maintain. One day, she insists: "I love horses; I want to ride." (It's remarkable how the most dysfunctional member of the family, the person that cares the least, can suck all the oxygen out of the room and exercise dominance!)

My parents spot an ad in the *Grand Rapids Press*: "Help Wanted: Assistant at Riding Stable – Rockford". She settles in at the ranch, fifteen miles to the north, along with the other stable hands, and learns the ropes: harnessing, saddling, grooming, and riding the trails with paying customers.

After several weeks, my parents express concern about her wellbeing. Dad calls the rancher: "Can her younger brother join her and help out? – free of charge." The reply: "Of course; bring him over. He can stay two weeks." *I am sent there to spy! Well, why not? (That's the quintessential American question).* My dad spent two years in the Dutch cavalry, grooming and riding horses. Should be fun; won't hurt to see what it's like. *It smelled, that's what!*

Dad drops me off at the ranch. It looks like the hollers of Appalachia, weathered and ill-maintained. I enter a totally alien subculture – the kind which loves to hang out at the seedy bars and sidewalks of Commerce Avenue. Night after night, I endure endless profanity, indignities, drinking, and rowdiness. This is not my universe. Charles Bukowski would feel at home here, not me!

During the second week, my sister confides to me: "Guess what? The old man (they were a childless couple) told me he wants to have sex with me, so they can have a child!" And would you believe, next day, the old reprobate tells me the same thing he told her. No shame! I waste no time, contact my parents; and we whisk her out of the dregs.

Shortly thereafter, something hit the news that would linger in headlines for years. A local Dairy (which, incidentally, delivered the weekly block of ice for our "ice box", back in 1950, with their horse-drawn wagon) was caught in a nefarious scheme. Purportedly, as a side enterprise, they processed meat – often from cattle that weren't slaughtered, but picked up dead in barns and fields.

The scandal sparked outrage, bitter protests and lawsuits. The prime mover of this fraud and misery? You guessed it: Roy, the sleazy horse rancher! He was about sixty years old when he made his indecent proposal to my sister. He had perpetrated his dead-cattle scam for years, before being found out.

What happens to my sister? She begins running off with lowlifes. My mother pleads with me, "John, bring her home!" It falls on me to rescue her from dens of iniquity. (Later on, I could easily relate to the plot and characters of Paul Schrader's film *Hardcore*, 1979). I repeatedly bring her "home". And no sooner does she recuperate from pennilessness and starvation, when she vanishes into the night. We even hire detectives to determine her whereabouts.

At one point, Dad buys her a quarter horse, boards it in the country (now, the city of Kentwood), hoping it'll help. It does, for a short while; but I am the one destined to ride and care for it. Finally, fed up with this equestrian diversion, and all those sleuthing and rescue operations, I bellow: "Enough of this horse shit!" (Today we call it "codependency").

I come home one day, about to air my frustrations – concerning the futility of our efforts. And, wonder of wonders: synchronicity. My mother has just spent the last hour crying profusely in her bedroom. She emerges and declares: "I prayed earnestly. I thanked God for the gift of my child, but I can't be a parent to her anymore. I have just given her over to Him, completely. He's her parent now. A burden has dropped from my shoulders, from my mind, from my soul. Now, John, you must do the same. She's no longer your responsibility."

"But she is!"

"No, she is not."

We embrace, and weep. We sell the horse, and put the emotional roller coaster behind us. We emerge as new people.

It is our Easter, a time for new beginnings.

CHAPTER THIRTEEN.

PORN KING

Half way back from Detroit to Grand Rapids in 1961, that old '53 Dodge coupe of mine throws a rod, and we cripple our way to an offramp gas station. I sell it on the spot for $25 and hitchhike home.

A seemingly decent, though grubby-looking fellow invites me to ride with him. He talks incessantly, telling me about his great plans to sweep the GR market with something he already has going in Detroit – a couple of specialty movie theaters. He plans to scout Division Avenue.

I hadn't revealed my background or beliefs, when he exclaims: "I'm the King of Porn! I'm on my way to conquer Grand Rapids."

Good grief! I don't know whether to tell him to stop and let me out, or if I should stay, just listen, and pry into his specific goals and strategies. I choose the latter. He inquires which hip radio station he should visit upon arrival, to place future ads. I reply: "Well, I know just the place – it ought to provide exactly what you need. By all means, visit WFUR."

"Wow, thanks. I'll get right on that." He drops me off, again thanking me profusely. I only wish I had been present when he walked through the door of that Christian family radio station!

A year later, working part time for the *Grand Rapids Press* Advertising Department, who walks up to my counter? You guessed it – pornmeister Floyd Bloss. He didn't recognize me, looked rather unkempt, smelled of booze, asking me to place an ad for his vice. I replied, "Sorry, company policy: we don't run that kind of ad." He stormed out, with choice words echoing from distant walls. Floyd Bloss was a Larry Flynt before Larry Flynt. He filled the air with controversy for decades to come.

For me, it was another 'Forrest Gump moment', as Grand Rapids culture hurtled relentlessly toward the abyss.

But something happened shortly after that initial encounter which restored my faith in humanity. It has to do with Richard – from a financially challenged family. I'll never forget the day I pick him up for school (high school carpool). His face is beaming. He was always a great kid, but his life was not always easy. His father was a short-fused, harsh, abusive alcoholic. His mother tried to hold everything together. That day, he is on cloud nine.

"Now listen guys," he warns, "don't laugh, because I did something I thought I'd never do. I bought my mother a ready-made dress from Herpolsheimer's. All her life she's been sewing her own; and she's scraped together every extra dollar to help pay my tuition and books. So, I did some saving of my own – and today's her birthday!

"I've rarely seen her cry tears of joy, but they sure flowed this morning. And, would you believe, the dress fit perfectly; she even loved the style and the feel. What's not to be happy about?"

At that instant all goes silent. We swallow our chuckles; and somehow we sense that this is a sacred moment.

I remember Richard as a living example of gratitude; and I'll never forget the joy he radiated.

There was still much goodness in Grand Rapids.

CHAPTER FOURTEEN.

ANYTHING GOES

chool Year 1960-61

S   Enamored of media, I would peddle my bicycle through the beautiful wooded campus of Aquinas College to its radio station. I ask Father Mike, popular with young people of all faiths, if I can be in the room during his live broadcast. "Okay John, just sit on the floor right over there; enjoy, listen and learn." Exposure such as this inspires me to apply for a most unusual one-time-only opportunity provided by Junior Achievement and WOOD-TV (studio on College Avenue) – a half-hour show produced by teenagers, for teenagers, every other week, just before the featured NBC Saturday afternoon college football game. Black-and-white TV – Live! Twenty of us are selected out of a huge pool of applicants from each of our city high schools, and we name our company *Tele-Teen Productions*.

We sell our own commercials, write our own scripts, build our sets, plan minute-by-minute floor traffic (so the cables of the three expensive in-studio cameras don't tangle). We audition a broad spectrum of teenage talent from each of our high schools and select, among others, contortionists, magicians, singers, instrumentalists, and comedians. We deliver our own high school news, sports and interviews.

During the first semester of that 1960-61 school year – when John F. Kennedy is elected and inaugurated President of the United States – we are on air Live. (Speaking of butterflies, nerves! No room for errors.) Second semester, WOOD-TV purchases three new RCA video tape machines, huge units, with tape three inches wide. We tape our show Thursday night (we can do retakes), then sit at home and watch ourselves perform early Saturday afternoon.

Just shy of fifty-thousand viewers tune in to the variety show we christened *"Anything Goes"*, heralded by the musical intro of the Broadway hit by the same name. The station's director, behind studio glass, has the fortuitous name "Wild", so we sign off every program with the tag "This has been a Wild production!"

When it's a wrap, crews set up the studio for a kids' show – talented cowboy Buck Berry, and his "Buckaroo Rodeo", locally more famous than Buffalo Bob. Kids adore him, even though he often stutters and stumbles his way through. TV is in its infancy – one grand adventure.

In 1960, some Christian families are still conflicted about television in their homes, but they too are swept along by the currents of history – which Orson Welles summed up so well in 1956: "I hate television. I hate it as much as peanuts. But I can't stop eating peanuts."

December 7-9, 1961: The annual YMCA Youth Legislature convenes in Lansing, Michigan. One hundred fifty high schoolers, mentored by elected officials, 'take over' the reins of State Government.

Dave and I represent Grand Rapids. Needing a bill to submit to the House, we come up with the idea of offering a tax credit to homeowners building a fallout shelter on their property. An attorney volunteers to help us formulate the bill.

Alas, it dies an unceremonious death as it struggles its way through various committees. Our peers argue that, upon emerging from said shelters, you'll be irradiated anyway; furthermore, there are needs in society more urgent than mere individual self-preservation. They're right, of course.

The world of politics is laid bare to us. We learn by doing, and discover that government works if you have the will to make it work. It takes guts, perseverance, brains, genuine concern for the commonweal, willingness to listen, to compromise on matters that are negotiable – and it doesn't hurt to have a law degree and lots of friends.

What moves us deeply is the Joint Session of the House and Senate, December 8, 1961, 1:30 pm. All eyes are fixed on the forty-second Governor of the State of Michigan, Canadian-born Honorable John B. Swainson (1925-1994) as he walks down the center aisle of the House floor, up to the podium, on artificial legs – without crutches or support – to address us. He exudes confidence and joy. He had been the captain of his high school football team; then lost both legs as a teenager, age nineteen, in France during World War II. All of us were awestruck. He was in our eyes a true hero.

As a double amputee, he refused to be held down by his handicap. In his meteoric rise to political power, having served in the State Senate, and as Lieutenant Governor under G. Mennon Williams, he was swept into the governorship at age thirty-five, on the coattails of an equally popular and charismatic candidate for President, John F. Kennedy. He truly "walked tall on his artificial legs", as one commentator put it; and we looked up to him. Such moments are seared in my memory.

His story is well told by Lawrence Glazer, *Wounded Warrior*, 2010 – about his two successful years as Governor, 1961-1963 (coinciding with the State's Constitutional Convention, and with JFK's abbreviated term in office), and his election to the Michigan State Supreme Court. Having served faithfully for twenty years in all three branches of government, he fell from grace in 1975 accused of bribery and lying to a federal grand jury (they rushed to judgment, not having heard all the eyewitnesses!) What followed were years of alcoholism and depression.

John B. Swainson disappeared into the shadows – but could not be held down forever; he possessed bouncebackability, becoming the highly-respected President of the Michigan Historical Commission – his honor fully restored. *"A just man may fall seven times, but will rise again."* *Proverbs 24:16*

CHAPTER FIFTEEN.

MY HERO

Every kid needs a hero. Most kids find them in the world of sports (football, baseball), entertainment (music, movies), or *Marvel Comics*. I find mine right at home – my older brother Ted, born 1934 (I tag along in 1943). He is totally in love with life, exuberant, full of talent – in sports, music (mimics Mario Lanza and succeeds), science (driven by insatiable curiosity), entertainment (wanting to make people laugh – like Robin Williams in *Patch Adams*, 1998). His positive energy brings sunshine where there is shadow. He will not be outdone; second-best is never an option!

Upon immigration to Grand Rapids in 1950, Ted is hired as one of the first employees of Meijer's Super Market, Eastern Avenue. He wastes no time buying a car, indulging his passion for sailing, and flying small aircraft in and out of Kent County Airport, off 28th Street. Ted is eager to show me the wonders of our new city. We slip into a back pew at a Wednesday night Black church service. Never heard anything like it! Before we know it, we're rockin'-n-rollin', swayin'-n-dancin' in a highly-charged emotional atmosphere. He takes me to venues where the greats play the mighty pipe organ, from Virgil Fox holding forth at Fountain Street Church – to the Majestic Theater and its Wurlitzer, played before and after the movie (for example, *Annie Get Your Gun*, 1950, starring Betty Hutton), but especially during an extended Intermission (a lucrative time for concessions).

Ted takes me to *Grand Rapids Rockets* games (International Hockey League) at the Stadium Arena (now the DeltaPlex), where we sit under a precariously sagging roof, crossing our fingers it won't collapse! At the landmark Civic Auditorium, we see side-splitting hypnotism-as-entertainment, the Shrine Circus, Harlem Globetrotters, plus incredible travelogues (before TV and Cinerama steal their thunder): large screen, full color, slow motion and time-lapse photography, exotic settings – like a virtual *National Geographic*. And there is Soft Water Lake, a fantastic diving venue, with its muddy water, mucky bottom, fish constantly brushing our legs, and a huge scary swing (which I avoid). My brother is a show off; he climbs to the top of the tower (a dizzying height) and keeps attempting the perfect swan dive, to impress the opposite sex. There's no stopping him – until….

He falls victim to the ongoing TB (tuberculosis) epidemic! - immobilized for two full years, at Sunshine Sanitarium (1952-54). His nurses are marvelous; they become like family. He spends endless hours building me a huge model airplane out of toothpicks, light paper and glue. He spends even more time preparing for college.

He and his fellow inmates, however, do get restless and mischievous on occasion. John Hockenberry (in the anthology *Thin Ice*, 2007) relates his own experience at Mary Free Bed Hospital – an uncanny parallel to what happens at Sunshine: "We were all fucked-up in some way. We hated the food, and we were all trying to beat the system. Days were spent trying to sleep in, slip out, obtain contraband, obtain privacy, simply gain a few moments of freedom. It was us versus them. We had the most fun. The staff held all the cards…. We kept things lively. They always won."[4]

My brother's sojourn through Sunshine impels him to become a physician; he wants to 'pay it forward'. At Calvin College, he helps establish an independent soccer club, becoming its captain and goalie. He and his Canadians play the newly-minted Big Ten teams (Purdue, Northwestern,

---

4   John Hockenberry, "A Farewell to Arms," in *Thin Ice* (Grand Rapids: Eerdmans, 2007), 326.

University of Michigan…) and come out Number One several years in a row! All that 'apprenticeship' by Dutch national champion Abe Lenstra, our next-door neighbor in Heerenveen, pays off!

Ted, some years later, sits on the bench with the Dallas Tornadoes (soccer) and Dallas Cowboys as an attending physician. He sings tenor in the Opera and Master Chorale, and invites me to watch him perform surgeries (with permissions, of course). I can't believe how calm he is under great stress.

But little am I prepared for the news that reaches me in 1971 while at work in the Yucatan Peninsula of Mexico. Four private planes piloted by volunteer physicians from Dallas (sixteen doctors in all), had flown to an isolated town in the hinterlands of Sonora, Mexico, to supply much-needed medical care. The first three planes landed smoothly on its dirt runway, but as the fourth made its descent, an enormous gust of wind tipped it upside down, causing it to crash. One doctor was killed outright; another ended up in a permanent vegetative state; yet another walked away with only a broken bone and some bruises; and my brother: half his body was crushed – from head to toe. Miraculously, he lived!

Colleagues medevac them back to Dallas. Dozens of specialists operate on Ted over a year and a half – complex restorative and reconstructive surgeries, using artificial parts, body tissue, transplants…, trying to put Humpty Dumpty back together again. I can't imagine what it must be like having to go through the pain, the endless procedures, the recovery, the readjustments – not only to come out looking halfway decent, but learning to walk again, regain his coordination, eyesight, voice, reflexes and stamina. Through all the agony, he wills to live, to overcome, to start afresh and blaze new trails. After all, you are the product of your choices. The last thing he wants is pity! Empathy, yes; pity, no. He is now the true *"Six Million Dollar Man"*.

He takes up competitive tennis, regains his voice and sings once more, marries a multi-talented woman, who herself has overcome insuperable obstacles and becomes *Ms. Senior America 2002*. Heaven, right? Indeed.

But with every gain, new pain. Life happens! Ted's oldest daughter, student at the University of Texas, Austin, is stabbed dozens of times by a violent intruder. Her little yappy dog becomes a loud, continuous alarm that alerts neighbors. They come running, scare off the monster, and rush her to the ER. Amazingly, she lives! Soon thereafter, Ted's oldest son is killed in a motorcycle accident.

Inconsolable? Of course. What more can happen? I don't know how, but again he recovers. He keeps doing surgery after surgery on others, saving them, relieving their pain and misery – which in itself makes for self-healing. My brother is indeed a 'wounded healer', a true hero.

My brother George (eleven years my senior) is another in my pantheon of heroes. After receiving a 'Golden Parachute' from the Keebler Corporation, he became acting head of the (Grand Rapids) Kent County Red Cross. For years, he voluntarily flew around the world helping organize disaster relief efforts for the American and International Red Cross (Africa, Haiti…).

Perhaps each of us can be a hero to somebody else. In the words of Dr. Seuss: *"To the world you may be one person; but to one person you may be the world."*

CHAPTER SIXTEEN.

WHITE SOCKS

Summer 1964

S   With racial tensions brewing, Lyndon Johnson and Robert McNamara plotting to escalate the Vietnam War, the Beatles storming America (sparking cultural brouhaha: sex, drugs, eastern gurus, rock-n-roll), new rumors that "God is dead", and the New York World's Fair inviting us into a brave new scientific future (*Whew!*), and after two years of college, weariness and cabin fever: *I'm out of here! Europe, here we come!*

College made me an avid reader and bibliophile, but now I'm onboard Icelandic Airlines, itching to explore new worlds, meet fascinating people and ask lots of questions – the primary way I've learned anything important in life, other than adversity, or putting my hand to the plow.

Forty-five minutes out of New York our aircraft, a four-propeller wonder, begins tilting, then vibrating. I glance out the window and, horror of horrors, the far left engine is totally engulfed in flames! Passengers panic. The biology professor seated next to me (who had exhorted me never to write a textbook "because all you'll be doing the rest of your life is revising it") grabs the stewardess: "Get me a drink – now!" He isn't the only one. Soon it's drinks on the house.

"This is it," I muse, "we're fish food!" as the nun in front of me scribbles a final farewell. The pilot dumps thirty-thousand pounds of fuel into the ocean. And while inebriated passengers make merry, we bump and bounce our way back to JFK. Nothing like a little drama to launch a tranquil summer!

My trusty motorbike whisks me through city, hill and vale, from hostel to hostel (23 cents per night). On July 11, strolling along the river Main in Frankfurt, I relax on a bench – when a pair of menacing, grubby streettoughs walk up to me. My instincts say: *Run!* I've never run so fast! I storm breathlessly into the Youth Hostel, and tell the Director. After a pause, he looks at my feet: "John, you're wearing white socks!"

"Yeah, so?"

"Around here white socks mean: you're gay; you're available; you're ready for action!"

"Those guys looked threatening!"

"They are; they're ex-cons."

So I tear off those white socks, throw them in the garbage. Resolved: from now on, Dark Socks Only, and no more unwitting invitations to thugs versed in the vile arts of coercion and control! Do I hate gays? Absolutely not! I hate violence.

Next morning, Sunday July 12, 1964, 9:00 am, recovered and refreshed, I am about to have another *'Forrest Gump* moment'. I ring the front doorbell of the Frankfurt Mormon Mission House – hoping to reconnect with two bright, charming young ladies I had met on Icelandic Airlines. My relatives showed them two days of Dutch hospitality; they, in turn, invited me to chauffeur them all summer. With regret, I declined. (*'Concupiscence'*, said St. Augustine – avoid even the appearance of impropriety). *Dang!* Oh well, I also wanted freedom of movement. If we failed to cross paths, we agreed to meet here today.

A stern, puritanical house mother (Flora) answers the door. "The girls are not here". She assumes I'm up to no good (as in: *Leave our Mormon virgins alone!*) She says: "You better come in and talk with my husband."

(Subtext: *He'll straighten you out*). So she leads me through this magnificent palatial residence, through ornately carved oak double doors into what looks like the Oval Office. And before me stands – would you believe – Ezra Taft Benson, controversial Secretary of Agriculture under President Dwight D. Eisenhower. He's currently head of the European Mission of the Latter Day Saints (assigned there apparently because he became a staunch member of the John Birch Society, forerunner of the Tea Party and its offspring – a public embarrassment for the Mormon establishment at the time).

For half an hour we sit discussing theology and world affairs. (His voice inflections are like those of Gerald Ford). He listens, shows great respect, is engaging and congenial. Soon it's time for him to teach a class at his Stake; and before parting, I mention, "One of the first programs our family listened to upon immigrating was 'Music and the Spoken Word' with the Mormon Tabernacle Choir; we still listen today." (The following year, the Latter Day Saints decided to double their funding for the Choir). Remarkably, throughout our friendly exchange, he said hardly a word about those young ladies! Twenty-one years later Benson, as one of the Council of Twelve, was chosen President ("Prophet, Seer and Revelator") of the multi-billion dollar Mormon Church.

Before returning home that summer, I revisit the place of my birth. About to cross a narrow canal, I notice the bridge is out and people treading cautiously over makeshift boards (one-way foot traffic). A mother is busy warning her young daughter to be extremely careful walking the plank – when suddenly an elderly woman with a bicycle stumbles, almost slipping into the water. Our hearts skip a beat, ready to jump in and save her. Immediately, the precocious daughter addresses her mother (recalling what her mother was trying to teach her): *Voor de oudere jeugd is het beslist niet vertrouwd!* (Hilarious) - "For older youth it is *absolutely* unsafe!"

CHAPTER SEVENTEEN.

THE FLOOD

In my youth, I heard several candidates for public office campaigning from a makeshift platform near the front steps of the old Calvin College Administration Building, on Franklin Street. This venue was a hotbed of Republican orthodoxy!

I remember, however, how questions of party affiliation completely melted away in February of 1953. The Auditorium of that main building was packed night after night to watch the black-and-white documentary *De Ramp*, about the breach of the dikes and devastating flood that inundated the Dutch province of Zeeland on January 31, 1953.

Over 1800 people drowned; 70,000 homeless; scenes of dead cows floating downstream. It was a collective shock, especially to our large immigrant community. Just coming to see the film was considered an act of solidarity; it was all quite spontaneous. Money was raised in large amounts at each showing for families of the victims.

To a nine-year-old kid, seeing these images was as disturbing as watching footage of the Holocaust. Forces of nature proved to be as calamitous as the destructive forces of history.

As a Calvin College Senior in 1966, I was selected to address faculty and students in Chapel. (It was a full house and a captive audience – only because Chapel was compulsory!) I reflected on that 1953 Flood and on Noah: 'In this very auditorium, as a child of nine, I sat alongside atheists and believers, Protestants, Catholics and Jews. We saw raw footage of death and devastation, which shook us all to the core. Party and religious affiliation no longer mattered. We were one, with a common concern. Together, we formed a rainbow that signaled hope. In our denomination today, perhaps the time has come to shed our exclusiveness, throw wide open the windows – as the Second Vatican Council has done – and embrace a more ecumenical future.'

Unfortunately, those in power were not yet ready for this kind of talk, or walk. I used the men's room afterward and noticed a sign above the urinal: *"We aim to please, so please aim!"* Well, I aimed straight in my address, but apparently did not please.

CHAPTER EIGHTEEN.

THE JOURNEY

rand Rapids 1960s

G There was a time when preachers were held in high esteem, especially in our *little "Jerusalem"*. The premier pulpiteer of the 1940s to 1970s (1944-79) was Dr. Duncan E. Littlefair (1912-2004), Fountain Street Church (founded 1869), the true Liberal voice of reason in a sea of authoritarian religion. *"I consider it my place not to dispense truth, but to stimulate inquiry,"* he said. (December 31, 1967 sermon)

I enter the sanctuary, ears attuned to magnificent music, eyes focused on translucent stained-glass images of Plato, Leonardo da Vinci, Charles Darwin, Erasmus, Washington, Jefferson, and Lincoln, alongside heroes of Biblical myth.

As lights are dimmed and all is quiet, I am embraced by a slightly raspy yet calm hypnotic voice painting word-pictures, stimulating my mind, eliciting emotions, stirring my soul. This meticulous scientific scholar with artistic bent transports me into the drama of another time and place, an ancient universal biblical story which magically becomes my story, with feet fixed firmly on twentieth-century soil.

I'm not talked down to, or made to feel guilty or afraid. My dignity and worth are affirmed, while challenged to perceive the world through a new lens. As I discover fresh connections, my mind constructs new meaning. This is naturalistic religion at its best. There are no absolute answers to any questions; there is no 'supernatural'; no one speaks for another; no one speaks for God; God is totally incomprehensible; all reference to 'God' is metaphorical.

I'm not told what to think or do; I'm simply invited to join the speaker on his journey so I can launch out on my own. I don't accept anything because he says so. I must test and prove all things for myself. The primary function of religion, he says, is to help bring order out of chaos, to make sense of life. The question for me becomes: what will I do when I leave these premises and the ether wears off?

My mother comes from such a tradition (Dutch Reformed Church, The Netherlands – which scrapped all obligatory creeds and confessions in 1830), emphasizing love-of-neighbor: do all you can, individually and collectively, to make this world a better place – more just, truthful, peaceful. Accordingly, she was irenic, ecumenical, open to truth wherever it may be found, non-judgmental, non-dogmatic, supportive of women's equality and human rights. I am my mother's son religiously, more than my father's (confessional 'Christian Reformed').

And yet, I want to become a leader in a dogmatic, restrictive Christian Reformed Church! Yes, because it's what I was raised in, what I know, what I want to help reform. I'd like to see it open up to the world, no longer running roughshod over individual conscience.

The second prominent preacher of the era is Dr. David Otis Fuller (1903-88), Wealthy Street Baptist Church (founded 1886), a dynamo, holding forth forty years (1934-74) – the polar opposite of Duncan Littlefair. Wealthy Street becomes a hotbed of American Revivalist Fundamentalism, a megachurch of its day, much like Charles Haddon Spurgeon's Tabernacle in London and Dwight L. Moody's Church in Chicago. Its focus is the less-educated working class, individual conversion, authoritative dispensing of eternal truths, strict adherence to a set of prescribed beliefs, walking the straight-and-narrow – enticed by the reward of heaven and the fear of hell! The fainthearted and gullible surrender their intellect at the church door.

These two pastors, these two churches, are lightning rods of the momentous Liberal-Fundamentalist Conflict in America. Grand Rapids is a microcosm, a laboratory. D.O. Fuller hurls thunderbolts at 'Littlefaith', accusing him of blasphemy, communism, atheism and other '-isms'. Tolerant Littlefair declares: 'The only attitude I cannot tolerate is intolerance; but I'll continue preaching and living love the best I can'. Ironically, his nemesis - Wealthy Street - began as a mission outreach of Fountain Street in 1875. Mother and daughter had a falling out.

Amazingly, they do agree on something: they condemn Norman Vincent Peale's gospel of prosperity and success. They find *Peale appalling, but Paul* (in different respects) *appealing*.

To hear D.O. Fuller preach is to participate in a thrilling rhetorical event. I am swept away by his boundless enthusiasm, confidence and conviction. Regrettably, I'm not given space to pause and think for myself. I have to decide then-and-there between his way or the Devil's. No room for ambiguities, questions or doubts.

Do I respect him as a person, a fallible human being like myself? Of course. I sit in his study for hours (1967), discussing Evangelical Awakenings in American history and their influence on church and society. This is his area of expertise. In appreciation for my challenging questions and lively exchange, he gives me a copy of his anthology *Valiant for the Truth* (1961), and boldly asks me: "How do you know you're saved?" *What's wrong with this question?!* His answer is: "The Bible tells me so". And before saying farewell, he drives home his belief with a poem: *"All efforts to destroy are vain/God's Holy Word will still remain/So hammer on, ye hostile hands/ Your hammers break, God's anvil stands!"*

He follows up with a personal two-page, single-spaced typed letter, which concludes with his heart's sincere desire: "We need a revival that will spread all over this city and state and nation, for this is the one thing, John, that will ever keep America from complete and total chaos and catastrophe worse than any nation in any age of history has ever experienced."

Today, we would call this Trumpian hyperbole. The tables have turned. His fundamentalist heirs have helped create the chaos, not prevent it! The Salvation Industry has grown dramatically since the advent of modern communication, especially television, satellite and internet. Religious entrepreneurs are milking trusting souls dry, while living like drug kingpins. Early revivalists used Guilt as their preferred tool of manipulation; today it's Greed. Either way, they're picking pockets. Humans are religious by nature and easily duped. Cons come in many disguises. And the masses (mostly good people) have been encouraged by imposters to support candidates, now public office holders, who in fact work against the interests of the many, in favor of a few rich - while violating established law and basic moral norms associated with advanced Western civilization, including ' Christian morality'.

Dr. Littlefair was prescient in stating: "The crowds who surround demagogues...are those trying to escape the feeling of being nobodies"; they want to feel important; they want to be noticed. (*The Glory Within You*, 1973)[5]

Wealthy Street Baptist is now defunct. The Bible Institute D.O. Fuller kick-started in his church basement (1941), however, has endured – as Cornerstone University. Fountain Street Church, though graying and diminished in numbers, remains a powerhouse in the arts and social justice.

As I write this, on my journey, after decades of churchlessness, I am still Christian, but Christian only to the degree it embodies good religion, and religious only to the extent it embraces the truly human. As to Scripture: it is not the sole possession of church and synagogue; it belongs to all people everywhere as a common literary heritage.

I'll wrap it up with a favorite Littlefair benediction: "*Here's to the wonder, miracle, glory and joy of life!*"

L'chaim!

---

5   Duncan E. Littlefair, *The Glory Within You* (Philadelphia: The Westminster Press, 1973), 31.

CHAPTER NINETEEN.

FUNDIES

It's *June 1966*. "You're a Dutch Calvinist? You've only been sprinkled?" my new dorm-mates ask rhetorically. Out of the blue, they grab me, each taking an arm or a leg, haul me to the nearest bathtub and dunk me, fully clothed *(Evangelical hazing!)*; "'In the name of the Father, Son and Holy Ghost. Amen.' There, now you've been properly baptized. Welcome to MBI." Moody Bible Institute, it turns out, is populated with Baptists.

I wanted to feel first-hand what it was like to be a Fundamentalist student. So between Calvin College (1962-66) and Calvin Seminary (1966-69) I became a two-week guest of MBI, the mother of all Bible Institutes. 'Going to the source' means a dingy dormitory in a seedy section of Chicago – but then, everything has a price.

It becomes abundantly clear that MBI stands in the shadow of Dallas Seminary, the hotbed of "Premillennial Dispensationalism". They have precise timetables for the "End Times", popularized by Hal Lindsey in *The Late, Great Planet Earth* (1970). Its message, in a nutshell is: 'The world will be ruptured, and we ("the saved") will be raptured.' To hell with everybody else!

The father of these fabled fantasies? John Nelson Darby (1800-1882). His views came to dominate the *"Notes"* of *The Scofield Reference Bible* (1909) – the book which laid the ideational foundation of today's militant, conservative U.S. "Evangelical" movement.

MBI is big on *"The Fundamentals"*, promulgated in the early 1900s by reactionary conservatives at Princeton Seminary. The five non-negotiable fundamental beliefs are: Jesus' virgin birth, miracles, atoning death, bodily resurrection – and underlying it all: inerrant Scriptures, interpreted 'literally'.

At the Scopes Trial of 1925, their champion William Jennings Bryan voiced rejection of Darwinian evolution and a host of other 'isms' (naturalism, secularism, humanism, liberalism, syncretism). I find it curious that, at this stage of history, Fundamentalists made little objection to abortion – after all, it was a convenient way to diminish the black population!

That right-wing belief system all hinged on the Bible being the 'word of God' rather than the 'word of man', divine revelation rather than human creation, 'from above' rather than 'from below'. Knock over this kingpin, and all the rest of the pins fall with it.

Yet, as they sing *"How Firm a Foundation"*, most certainly, their *terra* is not *firma*. For in practice, all appeals to 'literal' Scripture yield infinite arbitrary and contradictory interpretations. My own position is this: *Every claim that something comes 'from above' actually comes 'from below'*. You can't get around this. Even theologian Bruce Springsteen, when interviewed, got it right: "Whatever we know about the divine begins with the human."

I try to figure out what makes these MBI students different from everybody else. Well, they're no longer in the gutter, drunk, stealing, gambling, smoking, swearing, womanizing…at least, not for the time being. They profess to have left these things behind, transitioning from vice to virtue, death to life, materiality to spirituality. I tag along on their daily mission outings; for example, street-corner evangelism on State Street. They have a circus barker stand on an orange crate, shouting something like "Hell's bells if you don't repent right now! And here's the payoff if you do…." Other students stand around pretending to be people drawn in from the streets, offering audible responses and interaction. It was all theater – a con, deception, trickery! Their rationale, of course: "The end justifies the means." What a sad joke.

In contrast, another group visits Cook County Psychiatric Hospital (Oak Park Avenue). It has the feel of a prison. Doors clang shut behind us with potent reverberations. Mingled with the smell of urine, we hear moans, shrieks, expletives, moronic laughter; an orderly shouts "Joe, put your horse back in your barn!" We're invited into the unit which houses the most hopeless and extreme cases. Luckily, they're under heavy sedation.

These women students (most of whose families had a member with mental problems) gently touch the patients, read to them and give them words of encouragement. I am strangely moved: no proselytizing, just love. When asked, "Why waste time on hopeless cases?" they respond: "You never know what gets communicated. Just do the right thing and leave the rest to God." Happily, within a rigid Fundamentalist camp, I had found the Liberal compassion of a Mother Theresa. *"Blessed are they who comfort, for they too have mourned."* (Peter De Vries, *The Blood of the Lamb*, 1961).[6]

Exiting the asylum, we hear one last blood-curdling scream: *Why-y-y?!* – It's the gawd-awful universal cry of despair. I picture him shaking his fist to heaven. Most of us can relate: it's that climactic burst of anger before disintegrating, and the future becomes a thing of the past. This dance of atoms needs release. The '*Why?*' has no answer, and it's not for the comforter to give one.

All that is needed to give comfort and support is our presence. Just show up. Next, shut up; remain quiet. As the saying goes: "People need to know that you care, before they care what you know."

I recall one plaque on the wall of that institution: "I'm absolutely crazy about change. I just can't handle it very well."

I also overheard a nurse shouting into the ear of an elderly ward: "Nelly, tomorrow's your 95th birthday!"

"Yeah!"

"But don't worry. You'll forget!"

---

6   Peter De Vries, *The Blood of the Lamb* (New York: Signet Books, 1963 softcover edition), 175.

CHAPTER TWENTY.

THE MOB

With a hand on her thigh, he whispers, *"Sometimes I think this leg is the most beautiful thing in the world, and sometimes the other; I suppose the truth lies somewhere in between."* (Peter De Vries, *The Blood of the Lamb*, 1961)[7]

De Vries knows that within the Dutch Chicago church of his youth, theological debates occasionally resolve themselves in similar fashion, but without the eroticism. For example, regarding the "End Times", which is more attractive? Premillenial Fundamentalism, or Postmillenial Liberalism? The Calvinist Amillenial sweet spot lies alluringly in between.

Dr. Edward J. Masselink (1901-1999) pastor of First Christian Reformed Church, Cicero, Illinois (1944-1950) is a brilliant proponent of this point of view on the airwaves of Chicago, a persuasive person of integrity.

Death threats are hurled at him! When elected president of the Cicero Ministerial Association in 1948, he decides to launch a non-violent holy war against the mob once run by "Scarface" Al Capone (1899-1947).

Cicero became Capone's lair in 1924 through election fraud, bribery and murder. Most citizens, out of fear, looked the other way as the crime syndicate tightened its grip on bootlegging, gambling and prostitution.

---

7   De Vries, *The Blood of the Lamb*, 27.

Masselink tirelessly mobilizes the faithful against boss rule - enlisting civic organizations, filing petitions, storming Town Hall, appealing to the Governor, Legislature and State Supreme Court. The racketeers, in turn, threaten our hero: "If that Masselink doesn't shut his mouth, we'll have him riding out of town on a slab!" (Robert P. Swieringa, *"Masselink Challenges the Cicero Mob"*, 2006)[8]

His life is in peril; yet, victory seems certain when a Circuit Court Judge orders the town board to call an election (for January 1950). On the ballot: Change Cicero from a town to a city. If it succeeds, the entire corrupt town board is dissolved.

Sadly, a dramatic reversal demoralizes our crusaders. The mob resorts to the mother of all dirty tricks: the race card! Residents of lily-white Cicero, who had fled Chicago's black inner city, are handed fliers at their front door by hulky hired black males, urging them to vote 'Yes' on the Referendum. Why? 'So blacks can move into the city'.

Needless to say, the once assured victory - by deception - turns into disastrous defeat. The bosses retain control; and for celebratory fireworks, they torch the personal property of the only black family in town – sparking a riot which brings out the National Guard!

Edward Masselink is a true profile in courage. Ironically, in practice, he is a liberal postmillennial – which means, the 'Kingdom of God' is something you bring on earth here-and-now primarily through your own action – much like Martin Luther King, Jr.

Eighteen years later, *1968:* It is a tumultuous year - assassinations, war protests, racial tensions, the Chicago Democratic National Convention.

All hell breaks loose in Cicero! The gifted, eloquent Rev. Eugene Bradford (1915-2010), champion of racial justice, and activist-heir to Dr.

---

8   Robert P. Swieringa, "Masselink Challenges the Cicero Mob," *Origins* 24, no. 1 (2006): 36.

Edward Masselink, leads the charge to integrate Timothy Christian School. Mob bosses retaliate with death threats, and Ebenezer Christian Reformed Church is polarized. Tensions are high – from within and without.

Cicero, the *"Selma of the North"*, has more guns and ammo stored in basements than any U.S. municipality! Blacks and minorities are allowed to provide services by day, but must leave town by dusk. No one dares integrate Cicero Public Schools. Even Cardinal Cody lacks the pluck to integrate Cicero Catholic Schools. The Capones have spoken.

Bradford, totally stressed, is granted a three-month sabbatical. He interviews seminary finalists for this plum summer assignment. I didn't apply. Last thing I need is trauma and danger! Besides, I'm getting married at summer's end.

Bradford calls me (he must have spoken with my landlord, Masselink): "John, I've spoken with your professors. They say you would be the best fit. You and I think alike; we share the same progressive social agenda." How could I say no? He: "It's all yours. Do your best."

The pews are packed every Sunday. The rapport is excellent. I'm there to build bridges, not polarize. I visit families in their homes and ask them point blank: "If you are zealous about integrating Timothy, are you willing to risk your own life to make that possible?" Only a few answer yes. Then I ask: "Are you willing to risk the life of your child to make that possible?" Not a single one answers yes. I have found common ground! Seeking a solution to a devastating dilemma hinges largely on how you frame the question.

Survey completed, I reveal my findings. Parishioners are surprised that their true feelings do not match their professed principles or ideals. "For what it's worth", I conclude, "I'm a realist; and if I had a stake in this community, I'd move the school to a nearby town that does not discriminate on the basis of race. I only echo a few good people who've already made this suggestion. You can have your school, integrate, and spare your child's life all at the same time – a win-win-win." Two years later, they moved Timothy Christian to Elmhurst.

Before my departure, I address the congregation: "I feel somewhat like John Howard Griffin, in *Black Like Me* (1961). The white author gets to feel what it's like living inside a black man's skin; but when he's done, he has the luxury of removing the shoe polish and goes home. I have immersed myself in your joys and struggles, and now I get to return to the safe haven of a seminary. You bear the heavier burden. But somehow, I trust, this summer has made each of us better people."

Fellow seminarian Joshua, fruit of our Nigerian mission, stands up for our wedding in the Chicago suburb of South Holland, (while Mayor Daly mobilizes his police force to commit aggressive acts during the Democratic National Convention). We receive anonymous phone calls with veiled threats: "Don't allow that darky into our church building, or else…!" We proceed with the wedding, and refuse to be intimidated.

That summer, the Christian Reformed Synod adopts Eugene Bradford's *"Declaration on Race Relations"* as official denominational policy. In the midst of turmoil, good things really do happen.

CHAPTER TWENTY-ONE.

AMO, AMAS, AMAT

*C*alvin *Seminary Autumn 1968*

    A catchy song hits the airwaves: *"Bend me, shape me, anyway you want me. You got the power to turn on the light.*[9] It titillates sexually, motivates spiritually. Take your pick.

I have seen the light academically. Many have. We will boycott all classes until our grievances are addressed. Down with impractical dogma! Out with antiquated pedagogy! Away with airs of exclusivity and superiority!

As we begin marching, the entire student body follows, circling the seminary complex once, twice – and somebody shouts: "Seven times! Jericho!" Then a third and fourth round: "Reformation! Change now! Relevance! Walk, not talk!" With the seventh revolution the walls do not tumble. *We forgot our trumpets!* Good news: the faculty caves in and accedes to our demands. Miracle? Perhaps. They don't want bad press. What's more, it's the sixties.

---

9   Scott English and Larry Weiss composed *"Bend Me, Shape Me"* in 1966. It was made famous by *The American Breed* in 1967.

Clinical Pastoral Education at Pine Rest Psychiatric Hospital has a semester opening. I jump in. The staff is awesome – wounded healers – vulnerable, tough, committed professionals. The best of them are still fighting their own demons and receive regular counseling. *It takes one to know one.*

Friends ask: "What are you doing in that looney bin? They're abnormal!"

"Aren't we all? We're all flawed, fallible carbon-based life-forms, on a spectrum of 'normality'. It's part of being human. But we are here to help each other."

I'm assigned two women with postpartum depression. One is extreme – under the delusion of having given birth to the Antichrist! This is clearly ideational, but what brought it on? A male megalomaniac thinks he's God! I read Milton Rokeach's *The Three Christs of Ypsilanti* (1964). Paranoid schizophrenia is a tough nut to crack. It's like the profile of a Jim Jones, a decade later (People's Temple, Guyana, 1978)

Students are told little about their assigned patients; we may not tape record or take notes. We are not therapists. Acting like one is illegal, even dangerous. After 45 minutes of clinical pastoral conversation, we sit for two hours and write a *verbatim* – documenting the entire session word-for-word as accurately as possible. Personal observation of body language, and opinions, are confined to the margins.

For therapists, our verbatim provides hints for healing. For seminarians, it's all about listening, especially *'active listening'* (something most of us are not good at). We realize quickly that the 'happy talk' of "positive thinking" is totally ineffective for deeply traumatized patients. It comes across as ludicrous insult. What we hear may be troubling, so I follow the rule: Stay engaged, but retain distance! Exiting the premises, I breathe a sigh of relief, and my own problems suddenly seem trivial.

We all need a healthy fantasy life. NASA scientists, for instance, are rational, anchored in reality, yet bathed in creative fantasy oriented to an open future. These institutionalized patients, in contrast, have lost touch with reality and live inside delusional fantasies. They've escaped the present and are frozen in the past.

Meanwhile, back at the seminary, a score of students spontaneously form sensitivity groups, based on pop psychology promoted by Thomas A. Harris in *I'm OK, You're OK* (1967). They spill their guts to each other – their dirty little secrets and frank opinions - only to be manipulated and betrayed! Several drop out of school in shame and anger. Two immediately file for divorce. Why? No professional guidance. They're playing with fire! The groups are promptly disbanded. Of one participant, I overheard a professor say to another, at graduation, "Let's just hope he doesn't do too much damage"!

I attend a performance of Mozart's *Requiem*, and sit next to a couple in their late 50s who look like homeless beggars. Hideous, repulsive. Her body is strangely twisted, missing an arm, loss of control in one eye. He staggers, is cross-eyed and weak. Mental deficiency?

I begin speaking with them, as I customarily do, and to my surprise they are not at all what they appear to be! After a lifetime of physical challenges, she had a massive stroke, and he, major heart surgery. But they glow! Warm-hearted, empathetic, great souls, well-read, finely-honed intelligence, eloquent, lovers of great music. They lost their life savings (which should never happen in this 'greatest of all nations'!), and a caring person gave them season tickets.

At concert's end, we sit and talk. The hall empty, she says, "It was so good to talk with you. No one has ever spoken with us at any concert; they all avoid us, but you engaged us; this is a first."

"You are both beautiful people," I respond. "I'm happy we could be together at this inspiring event, and enjoy it together." It's another unplanned encounter, as glorious as any that has ever occurred.

At Intermission, I had heard her reading the Latin text of the *Requiem* and commended her on her excellent diction. Asked if I took Latin, I launched into a euphoric "Oh yes, did I ever! I was a budding adolescent, tenth grade Christian High, and made a special request to sit front row center."

"You liked it that much?"

"No, but I fell in platonic love with the voluptuous teacher. I was mesmerized. What lungs! She was wonderfully buxom – a veritable Dolly Parton, and I had raging hormones. Transfixed by her heavenly charms, it was easy to chant the conjugations: *amo, amas, amat, amamus, amatis, amant....*" Apparently, our concert seat-mates had no problem relating to the phenomenon of adolescent libido, and burst out in laughter, arousing the curiosity of bystanders.

How good it was that my initial impressions of them were totally wrong!

CHAPTER TWENTY-TWO.

BRIDGE BUILDERS

On *October 31, 2017,* my dentist gives me *Novacaine* to prep for new crowns. My mouth is numb; I can barely speak. He starts talking about Halloween. *It's annoying when dentists gab while patients only grunt!* I want to remind him that today is the 500th anniversary of the Protestant Reformation – Professor Dr. Martin Luther (1483-1546) nailing those *"Ninety-Five Theses"* on the door of the campus church at Wittenberg in 1517, challenging the Catholic Church's sale of "Indulgences" ('Get out of Purgatory' certificates).

I try my utmost to get the words out: *We-mem-ba...Maht'n Lufa... when 'e hail'd doze 95 feces to d' do....* Well, that's how it came out! My dentist, usually sedate, bursts out laughing, and returns home content to be Catholic.

Ann Arbor, Michigan 1968

My mind flashes back to a time and place where Luther's tradition of protest is very much alive. Both church and state need decontamination. I'm determined to visit a lightning rod of social change, the dynamic (University of Michigan) campus ministry of First Congregational Church.

Founded 1847 in fierce opposition to slavery, the congregation also becomes a champion of women's equality, the right to vote, anti-Confederacy, anti-Vietnam War, pro-Civil Rights.

In 1830, runaway slave Josiah Hanson had already established himself across the river from Detroit in Dresden, Ontario. His farm, (later dubbed *Uncle Tom's Cabin*), becomes a destination for many more escaped slaves, freed from their misery by way of the "Underground Railroad". Rescuers risked life and limb for the cause; theirs was true religion in action.

Josiah Hanson, preacher and abolitionist, writes his influential autobiography in 1849.

Harriet Beecher Stowe publishes her novel *Uncle Tom's Cabin* in 1852 – becoming the bestselling book of the nineteenth-century after the Bible – which, besides the stirring rhetoric of Frederick Douglass, profoundly influences Abraham Lincoln, and solidifies Northern resolve both before and during the Civil War.

In 1853, Solomon Northrup's true story *Twelve Years a Slave* is published, in which he confirms from personal experience everything described in fictional form by Stowe.

Hanson's, Stowe's and Northrup's books together lead to a formidable tradition of protest literature in this nation. Within this living context, in retrospect, First Congregational is born.

The campus pastor leads me to the basement of the sanctuary, and says, "John, most people don't know this, and you won't find it published anywhere, but this is the very place where the radical movement of the 1960s was born! Some of the offshoots may have become anarchistic, which we reject, but it was all conceived and organized right here."

He continues, "SDS (Students for a Democratic Society), the New Left, spread rapidly from here throughout the nation – to campuses at Berkeley (CA), Columbia (NY), Madison (WI). Its initial focus was Civil Rights. With the escalation of the Vietnam War in the mid-sixties, and the influence of conscientious Quakers, its focus became anti-war, pro-peace."

As the Federal Administration keeps lying to the American people, SDS has a positive agenda, encouraging all-night "teach-ins" on U.S. campuses. It spreads like wildfire; this is the sixties at its best.

In 1962, Tom Hayden (1939-2016) (later married to Jane Fonda), a most admirable intellectual, who advocates for peace through non-violent resistance (in the footsteps of Mahatma Gandhi and Martin Luther King, Jr.) drafts a seventy-five page constitution for the SDS. He's one of the good guys, eventually becoming a popular progressive leader in both the California Assembly and Senate for sixteen years.

When I made that visit to Ann Arbor in 1968, it was the previous year that Detroit had gone up in flames. Rosa Parks, who lived in the midst of it all, agreed with Congressman John Conyers that "what really happened was a police riot". Young blacks without weapons were shot to death. After five days, over four-hundred buildings were burned. Discrimination had found its way from the South to the North, and Detroit has never been the same. (Identical problems linger on today!)

In August 1968, Hayden rightly stirs up holy hell in Chicago against the war in Vietnam, facing Mayor Daly's police mafia. Thankfully, conscientious resistance will one day prevail!

My Ann Arbor visit completed, I need some nourishment before returning to Grand Rapids. I stop at a popular campus restaurant, order my food, and ask four graduate students at a round table if I can join them. They say, "Sure, have a seat." Refreshing conviviality! Here are four young men and women – students in international relations, business, education and art – busy discussing their future, of all places, in China!

It is 1968, but China has been closed to the United States since 1949 – with no prospect that this *status quo* will change in the near or distant future. And yet, they are convinced, all signs to the contrary, that it will happen in their lifetime. They are of one accord. They see themselves as future cultural, economic and political bridge builders (literally, *pon-tif-ic-ators*) between East and West. All their academic preparation is geared to this single vision. I am spellbound. These students are true believers in things you can only hope for in your wildest imagination.

It was a long wait, but the change these harbingers of peace desired to see came true. Their endurance was richly rewarded.

CHAPTER TWENTY-THREE.

MISS MIMI

Calvin Seminary: Dies Natalis, March 1969
In seminary, I was put in charge of the student mimeograph machine (before PCs and laser printers!). I called her "Mimi", my Bohemian. In my farewell to her on this festive day of skits and monologues, I stand before an assembled faculty and student body, entrusting my office to a worthy successor.

"Gentlemen, on this auspicious occasion, allow me to wax sentimental and anthropomorphic. Authentic mimeography, inspired by the Song of Solomon, is a spiritual discipline not to be minimized. To you, Peter, I entrust the keys of the kingdom of Mimi; you will open doors for many.

"All I ask is – treat her as if she were your girlfriend! (*Raucous laughter! Totally unexpected. I'm not funny.*) Admire her sensuous symmetry; feel the texture of her skin; cuddle and caress her; whisper sweet nothings; don't be embarrassed; it's foreplay. And you'll hear her say: "Yes! Love me. All I need is love. Be gentle with me, and I'll put out for you. When you hear me humming, I'm enraptured, orgasmic, and all's right with the world.

"Please, don't abuse me, call me names or make me feel bad. Mimeos are people too. Value me; praise my good qualities; celebrate my achievements; make me feel safe and happy. And if you feel sad, go ahead, lay your head on my shoulder and cry.

"Peter, life can be beautiful; we can achieve great things together. Be passionate with me. I want action – lots of it; in fact, I can never get enough. Sniff my ink; set me in motion; bring out the best in me and listen to me hum. All you have to say is 'Ditto'.

"Don't be disappointed, however. Others may touch me. This relationship can't be exclusive. I was created to be promiscuous, ever available, a courtesan. Don't be jealous; it's my nature.

"And John, I bid you farewell. Thanks for the memories. We've produced numerous offspring, you and I."

"Well, I'm sorry we have to break it off now, Mimi. I'm closing the door on these fantasies. I'm going back to my wife, my one and only true love. I've learned from you that I must cherish her with patience and passion."

I forget what I told my soulmate that evening – something like: *"The greatest thing you'll ever learn is just to love and be loved in return."*[10] (Or, was that from *Moulin Rouge*, 2011?)

On that very night, our first child was conceived.

Cabin fever is stifling after seven years of college and seminary. An old adage describes the feeling well (translation mine): *"Cares which on the shore prevail, Set the longing ship a sail."* (Dutch: *"De wal van de dagelijkse zorgen van het leven keert meestal het schip van verlangen."*)

I graduate, and yet, with Goethe's *Faust*, lament (translation mine):

Well, doggone! I've studied philosophy, law, medicine, and even,
Bless my soul, theology. I've studied them all with ardent zeal;
Yet, here I am, a wretched fool with all my lore
No wiser than I was before.

---

10   Eden Ahbez, from his song *"Nature Boy"*, composed in 1947, and first recorded by Nat King Cole. The best rendition, without peer in my opinion, is by Jason Gould (son of Barbra Streisand); on *YouTube*, recording released on October 9, 2012.

(Da steh ich nun, ich armer Tor!
Und bin so klug als wie zuvor.)

Sounds like Plato. Faust and I need more than book learning. Latin
America beckons.

But first, peer examination for ordination: Indiana, August 1969. All goes
swimmingly – until it's time to deliver the sermon. My sponsoring church
just completed the construction of a new pulpit – high up, and extremely
remote from the congregation! "John, would you please mount the pulpit?"

"No, I'm sorry, I can't do that!" Whereupon, the majority of these
traditionalist examiners express shock. I explain: "That beautiful perch
may be perfect for my distinguished sponsors, but I'm called to stand in
the midst of people, close to them, on the same level."

Fury ensues! (Seven full minutes): "You're offending your host! Don't
you realize that the elevated 'perch' represents the supreme authority of
the Word of God?"

"I'm sorry; I'm a mere mortal, muddling through this life side-by-side
with you, trying to figure it all out. We're in this together. My ordination
gives me no greater authority to interpret the Scriptures than the janitor.
It only gives me permission." *I provoke. It's part of my calling.*

A lone progressive rises to my defense, saves the day, reminding this
august assembly: "He's a missionary, not a pulpiteer; he's not defying you
(as he tugs a ground-level lectern front-center - *Fait accompli!*). Grant him
his wish!" All are too flabbergasted to object.

Praise follows the sermon: "Hey, Mr. T, that wasn't half bad. Welcome
to the club." And they gave me my membership card.

LATIN AMERICA

1969–1972

CHAPTER TWENTY-FOUR.

MY MOBY DICK

an Jose, Costa Rica. December 1969

S   "This is paradise," I exclaim, as she guides me through the presidential estate. "Meet my husband, Don Pepe." Awesome! Don Jose "Pepe" Figueres (1906-90), hero of the 1948 Revolution - he overthrew a demagogue, abolished the military, gave women the right to vote and integrated *Tico* society.

First Lady (1954-58) Karen Olsen (born 1933), Danish-American Christian Science practitioner from New York, second wife (since 1954) of this legendary plantation owner, is a brilliant human rights activist – later, legislator and ambassador. We happened to meet at the only modern supermarket in town, "Auto Mercado". After a long conversation, she says, "John, come over this afternoon. I'll show you the furnished cottage we just completed on our estate, and your friends can have it for four months. After that, our estate will become the 'White House' again. We have no doubt Don Pepe will win this election by a landslide." And so he did!

We ourselves are comfortably settled in the residence of a wealthy businessman who's spending a year in Spain. The house includes their live-in maid, who not only does the cooking and cleaning, but becomes a key player in our cultural orientation to Latin America.

April 1970, immersed in Spanish language studies, a voice crackles over our Swan 350 ham radio transceiver, "John, I'm taking you to a three-day tarpon fishing contest, all expenses paid." I'm momentarily jarred: Is this what an aspiring missionary should be doing? The affluent ecclesiastical benefactor, intent on conquering the world for Christ and Capitalism, assures me we won't be struck dead for breaking the Sabbath.

Seated snuggly in a private Cessna, crossing the peaks between San Jose and the Caribbean coast, I state plainly, "All I ever fished was Reeds Lake and the Thornapple River."

"Don't worry. You'll get the hang of it. By the way, this trip for me is as much business as pleasure. Six Yanks in the tournament are scouting the tropical jungle for future resort development. Might take a while to pull it off, but…. We'll even build an airport."

Sudden turbulence jolts the fuselage. Dense fog envelopes our fragile shell. Unholy dread strikes us to the core. Which way is east, west? Up, down? The primitive landing spot beckoning us is a beach well off the radar.

My thoughts instantly conjure up a solo trek across the dome of Volcano Irazu two months earlier (no tourist safeguards). I was surreptitiously strangled by fog on a perfectly clear day while standing on a ledge overlooking the lava lake. With a visibility of twelve inches, I dropped on all fours and followed my footprints in the sand back to the road.

Now, in the face of imminent peril, our bush pilot yells "Don't panic! Pray." Whereupon, wonder of wonders, before us – a tunnel, a blue cylinder in the sky, a literal "window of heaven" materializes. *"Dive!"* I cry aloud.

Descending at a thirty-five degree angle through this celestial birth canal, we break out in doxology, circle the village of Colorado (five hundred souls), and land with a bounce on the beach. *We're saved – yet again!*

Village kids swiftly surround the plane vying to carry our luggage. We give each of them coins and candy, as our entourage, drenched in sweat, makes its way to the "hotel" by the river. We are on the edge of a jungle, waters populated by sharks and alligators. But however remote and dangerous, it is also the best tarpon fishing venue in the world.

Our hotel is a simple tree house on tall stilts – thatched roof, open door, open windows. (Beware tarantulas, poisonous walking sticks, or a boa constrictor curled up under your bunk). Outhouses are also up on stilts, strategically located over the bank of the river. Its flush system is the twice-daily high tide. If people are bored, they watch the action at the outhouse!

Our objective is simple: catch the heaviest tarpon (*Megalops Atlanticus*), the fiercest fighting fish in the tropics, with the lightest possible test line. A point-scoring system is used. Around Florida, anglers use a thirty to eighty-pound test line. The pros in this tournament use either eighteen or twenty-two pound lines, on a fly rod, with lures, girdled by a leather belt with a cup to hold the base of the rod. We decide to use a mere twelve-pound line – longer fight, but better odds of winning the cash pool.

And away we go! (the actual words on Jackie Gleason's tombstone) – in a long dugout canoe, with our indigenous guide at the stern, and a small outboard motor at hand. When we feel drained, our limber guide climbs the nearest palm, drops a few coconuts, slices them in half with his machete – *Voila!* – instant energy.

Beginner's luck. On the very first day, during the very first hour, in the lagoons off the Rio Colorado (connected to Rio San Juan, which divides Costa Rica from Nicaragua), something hits my line with explosive force and begins pulling us through the lagoon.

"John, hurry, get up to the front of the boat. Stay on your feet. Keep your rod down. Let it run. When you feel some slack, reel in the slack."

And so I did – when, in a flash, a powerful six-foot, 110-pound monster leaps high out of the water, with an electrifying shake, rattle and roll, its silvery side flopping back into its habitat. Then it sets out on another herculean run, pulling us along. Again I feel the slack. "Reel it in!" Another spectacular ascent into the air – like Bob Seagren doing the pole vault. The fight is on. Here is my *Moby Dick*, or Hemingway's Marlin off the coast of Cuba in *The Old Man and the Sea* – a formidable test of endurance. Which one will wear out the other first?

With luck, the hook anchors in one of the soft spots of the tarpon's jaw. (Usually, their mouth-made-of-bricks manages to spit out the hook after a couple of leaps). The battle persists– the leaping, the reeling, the long runs. And circling back to the boat, this denizen of the deep determines to tip us, or at least tangle our line. Smart creature. Sweat drenches my body. The struggle between man and nature wears on for over two hours. I am at the point of utter exhaustion. Soon, the rugged hauler maneuvers us out of the lagoon, into the wide river and toward the hazardous breakers of the Sea. Totally spent, I somehow manage to reel my *Nemesis* to the side of the boat – belly up!

Our guide places the gaffing hook next to its gill, ready to plunge it in (then haul it into the dugout and have it weighed on shore) –at which precise moment, I fail to realize my thumb is resting on the line. The giant abruptly jerks its head, snaps the line and vanishes into the vast murky unknown! *No-o-o-o!!!* After that enormous combat!! Man over nature? Nature outwitted man!

This was truly – I kid you not - the big one that got away. The exhilaration, the exhaustion; the excitement, the disappointment; the ecstasy, the agony; the adrenaline and the drop-dead bone weariness! After three days of jaw-to-jaw battles testing my reserves, it turns out that *Moby Dick* would indeed have won the prize. But that intrepid fighter had other ideas.

Strangely, in my heart of hearts, after the tournament was over and we all made it home intact, I was overcome with a profound feeling of contentment and joy that my worthy opponent outsmarted me and got away. It lived to see another day.

Already then, I began doubting my role as 'fisher of men'. Wouldn't the world be better off without the fish hook of Western imperialism? American literary critic Lionel Trilling wrote: *"Once we have made our fellow men the objects of our enlightened interest...we make them the objects of our coercion."* (In Joan Didion, *Slouching Towards Bethlehem*, 1968)[11] Ultimately, our target has a way of outsmarting us, eluding our grasp.

---

11   Lionel Trilling, in Joan Didion, *Slouching Towards Bethlehem* (New York: The Noonday Press, 1968), 162.

CHAPTER TWENTY-FIVE.

DEEP SEA

Perusing *National Geographic*, my mind flashes back to a '*Forrest Gump* moment' in 1970. On a flight from Guatemala City to San Jose, Costa Rica, a congenial adventurer carrying a sizeable wrapped object is about to take his seat next to mine. I comment: "You're holding that package as if your life depends on it."

"As a matter of fact, it does," he responds, "Would you like to see it?" Whereupon, the unveiling: "The latest and the best. I had it custom-made. And no, I'm not letting it out of my sight!"

"Goodness, this looks like something out of *20,000 Leagues Under the Sea* – the *Nautilus*, Captain Nemo, and all that."

Then comes the formal introduction: "I'm a deep-sea archeologist; I'll be doing exploratory work in the Pacific, off the coast of Costa Rica." He shakes my hand and says, "Hello, my name is Robert Ballard." His enthusiasm is contagious, as he clutches his weighty, spanking-new diving helmet. He's down-to-earth, easy to relate to, and remarks: "Interesting you should mention *20,000 Leagues Under the Sea*. It was the novel that thrilled me as a child and would never let me go; so, here I am today.

I remark, "I've read about the incredible finds of George Bass, who specializes in excavating shipwrecks of ancient civilizations."

"He's my inspiration. I stand on his shoulders. George is the father of deep-sea archeology."

Little did anyone know that Robert Ballard was only at the beginning of a long, illustrious career, soon to become a bright star in the firmament of exploration and discovery – with his find of the *Titanic*, the *Bismarck*, *PT-109*, ancient wrecks in the Black Sea…. Today we know the continuation of his daring story. It's almost as if, after such a fortuitous encounter, one has a personal investment in his success – even if the only investment is that of wishing him well.

On a flight a few years later, a fellow as huge as Bubba - of *Forrest Gump* fame - sits next to me in the aisle seat. Big Bubba had regaled Forrest with hundreds of different ways his Mama in the Bayou prepares shrimp: something like 'There's your shrimp gumbo, shrimp curry, Jambalaya, shrimp chowder, shrimp fajitas, shrimp bisque, shrimp creole' – which eventually leads to a *Bubba Gump* fortune.

I'm annoyed. My seatmate's corpulence severely limits the space I paid for in the middle seat. He's animated, friendly, knowledgeable in his interests, but every time he opens his mouth it blares like the Grand Haven foghorn. He retired young, and his passion is bees.

He proceeds, like Bubba, to list a thousand things one can do with honey. I shouldn't have opened the door – because, once wound up, he just couldn't stop! I'm thinking: *Bee kind; unwind.* After all, *a story - to be immortal - need not be eternal!* I'm hoping he'll make a visit to the bathroom. It doesn't happen.

After hearing about the nesting habits of (bee) drones and their relation to the queen bee, and the subdivision of colonies with the creation of a new queen bee, *ad infinitum*, I finally say: "Did you ever hear of St. Augustine?"

He replies, "Sure, it's that town in Florida."

"No, I mean the saint, the Church Father."

"No, never heard of him."

I said, "Well, Augustine loved bees and, like so many ancient authors before him, loved to use bees as an analogy to make an important point – not just that he had a honey of a wife, but as an illustration of both the providence of God (abundant provision), and as a model for human cooperation. But his personal passion was honey mead. After he drank it, he felt exceptionally relaxed and took his daily nap. Now, if you don't mind, I think I'll do the same."

It was quiet the rest of the trip. As we departed the plane, his wife (whom I didn't realize had been sitting in the middle seat in front of me) nudged me: "Thanks for shutting him up. I needed some shuteye!"

CHAPTER TWENTY-SIX.

THE DOORSTOPPER

M*ay 1, 1970*
 I board a Pan Am flight from Mexico City to San Jose, Costa Rica. In yet another fortuitous *'Gump* moment', the gentleman in the middle seat extends his hand: "Hi, I'm Eugene Nida." You've got to be kidding! - world-renowned linguist and translation guru (father of *"Dynamic Equivalence"*), American Bible Society, New York.

He sets aside his scribbled notebook (a new project on *"Semantic Domains"* – not published until 1988), and graciously engages me in conversation. I discover he was once a fundamentalist who, through meticulous scientific research and extensive field work, emerged as an ecumenist. His passion, like Luther (1522) and Wycliffe (1382), is to make the Bible available to people in their own language. He regards this venerable collection of books both as inspiration, and as a universal charter of freedom, self-worth, mutual respect, justice and peace.

He inquires, "What's that humongous book lying at your feet?"

"Fresh off the press," I respond, "old Reformed-scholastic dogmatic theology, translated into Spanish. I've been encouraged to use it with my future students."

"Ugh! That's the last thing Latin America needs!"

"This may surprise you, but I agree with you one hundred percent!" Whereupon I ask him, "What do you think it's good for then?"

He picks it up, and remarks, "Well, considering its weight and size, I think it'll make a great doorstopper!" *Hearty laughter.*

"In that case, what do you think the indigenous Maya of the Yucatan Peninsula really need, if we want to help better their lives?"

"You can start with *sex education*," he replies.

"No, seriously?"

"Absolutely! Start with practical down-to-earth stuff."

So I did. And – *Mama Mia!* – you can guess the reaction of my colleagues in Mexico City (ninety percent traditionalists)! I was forced to defend myself. Delegations were sent to determine if the scandalous rumors were true.

This is what they discovered: When students first heard about Sex Ed (a novelty in those parts), it generated instant enthusiasm. Even students' wives, siblings, parents and neighbors wanted in on this. Finally, I decided 'Come one, Come all', and we packed the hall to overflowing! The sheer number of participants revealed a widespread, burning, unspoken need. The Mexico City delegation couldn't put out the fire. Sorry guys. Get with the times.

We filled the coming years with cutting-edge courses and projects. And the impetus for all this? Dr. Nida's personal letter of encouragement a week after our encounter. Incredible, how 'your own people' can be naysaying obstructionists, while a helpful stranger takes the initiative to build you up.

So, how did it feel to be validated in this way?

It's like being inside an old story about the Pope.

As I chauffeur the Pope through Mexico, he says, "John, I'd really like to drive myself for a change."

"Okay," I respond, "but there's a notorious speed trap up ahead. Please don't speed."

The Pope speeds. He's pulled over by a trooper, who immediately radioes his supervisor.

"I just pulled somebody over who's pretty important."

"You didn't pull over the Mayor, did you?"

"No sir, he's bigger than the Mayor."

"The Governor?... The President?... Bigger than the President? My God, who did you pull over?"

"Well, I'm not exactly sure, but the Pope is his driver!"

·

CHAPTER TWENTY-SEVEN.

QUINTA EL OLVIDO

John Blodgett, son of wealthy lumber baron Delos Blodgett, built his *"Brookby"* estate – listed in the National Register of Historic Places – in East Grand Rapids (1926-27). The grounds were planned by the same architectural firm that designed Central Park in New York City and the Capitol Grounds in Washington D.C.

My dad (1901-81) is enamored of the beauty of these gardens, so having just retired, he knocks on John's (1901-87) door, asking him if for nominal compensation he could tend the flower gardens three mornings per week – with freedom to fish the private, adjoining Fisk Lake in the afternoon. John thinks it over: "You're on; welcome to the estate." My father is in seventh heaven, doing what he loves to do, for the next ten years.

I visit the estate often in the sixties. My favorite room in the mansion is, predictably, the library, with one of the finest private collections of United States history.

Merida, Yucatan Peninsula, Mexico. September 1970

I knock on Senor Quintero's door, richest man in town, to discuss a lease extension on his weekend estate, the national landmark *"Quinta El Olvido"*, built by thirty Italians in the late 1800s. It's a mansion on the edge of a city of 300,000 souls (now 1,200,000). All is approved.

The spacious mansion (photos online) accommodates our family, students, teachers, groundskeeper and kitchen staff (Yucatan Biblical Institute). Within its ornate walls, ceilings, floors and pillars, we hold our classes and sponsor retreats for up to 160 young people (each taking their own hammock).

During winter weeks, my dad helps Florentino tend the formal gardens and a myriad of fruit trees. Dad says, "I told Florentino to hold his head up high - that his work is as important as the Mayor's." He adds, "Remember, John, how when we first immigrated to Grand Rapids in 1950, a few people tried to make us feel second class? So I took you to Oak Hill Cemetery on Eastern Avenue, to the grave of my maternal grandmother (1845-1926).

"You were surprised to learn you had a great-grandparent who preceded us to the promised land. She was a widow with big dreams, arriving in GR in the 1880s - the boom years of its furniture industry – with one son and three daughters. (The daughter that stayed behind became your grandmother.)

"We have hundreds of relatives there whom we don't know. They contributed to the building of a vibrant city. They risked life and limb to rescue us in World War II. The effect of your great-grandmother's immigration came full circle. It doesn't matter if you're a Hollander or a Hottentot, we're called to be here for each other and build a new world together."

Our students at *El Olvido* live on a tight schedule: Up at six. Classes from eight to twelve. Noon dinner. Siesta. One hour labor in garden or mansion. Recreation. Study. Evening class in public school. Weekends: teaching and community development in assigned villages. Their commitment is exemplary, their enthusiasm contagious.

Many well-to-do *gringos* who support our foreign mission come to visit. Early 1971: We are asked to help orient and host two couples from Holland, Michigan – big contributors, who fly in by private aircraft. They're congenial personalities, and go-getters. We ask them about their business, community, church and family.

One of the couples mentions they have four children at home – among whom, Elizabeth age thirteen, and Erik age two. Would you believe? Our guests are billionaire industrialists Edgar and Elsa Prince. We had no idea at that time how politically conservative they were, that their daughter Betsy would one day marry Amway heir Richard De Vos, and become U.S. Secretary of Education in 2016, or that Erik would one day become a Navy Seal and establish the notorious Blackwater security firm (1997).

There is no doubt the Princes' have done much good with their wealth. But ideology has consequences. Erik, heir to Rambo and Oliver North, not only provided protection for diplomats in war zones abroad (*good*), but added 'mercenary' to his resume (*not good*). Four of his men, without provocation, opened fire on innocent civilians in Baghdad's *Nisour Square* September 16, 2007, killing seventeen. (The four perpetrators were at long last convicted, sentenced and imprisoned in 2014-15 for their crimes). Erik, who got off scot-free, became Steve Bannon's *(the loose cannon's)* secret weapon. He's the Prince sibling that really interests the current administration (2017).

But there is also questionable activity back then among Mexican authorities. My dad is shocked when on the first of each month police, fire and post office representatives stop by our front gate to collect their 'due' – protection money. If you don't pay? You may be robbed, have mail withheld, or something worse. Mafia? It's the system!

Neighborhood urchins regularly scale our fortress-like walls (on three sides), with shards of glass cemented into the peak, stealing fruit from our trees – in particular, the enormous mango tree that never stops producing. These are kids from extremely poor families; they're hungry. I don't want to see them get hurt; nor do I call the police.

So I ask Florentino what can be done. He suggests: "Have them come once a week, say Saturday morning at nine am, form a line at the front gate, and I'll give them their family ration for the week." "Great idea, Florentino. I'm putting you in charge of this operation." So, every Saturday a line forms, and every day our gardener sees the importance of his contribution. He's the new friend in the neighborhood.

Though lacking in education, Florentino is still a resident philosopher. Upon hearing about a gross injustice committed in our precinct, he radiates a sensibility that justice is somehow built into the fabric of history's cause-and-effect. He assures us all that, if the suspect is not convicted of his misdeed (It happens!), *"Don't worry, one day he'll fall down the well"* (a common occurrence in these parts) – his way of saying: ultimately, each will receive their due.

Life flourishes at *La Quinta*. The fruit is delicious, the pool refreshing, camaraderie stimulating and formation of hands-on leaders most gratifying.

CHAPTER TWENTY-EIGHT.

FRANCISCA

My Lai 1968

On March 16, 1968, U.S. soldiers slaughtered 504 unarmed Vietnamese civilians – elderly villagers, women and children at *My Lai*. Our military chain of command covered up this and dozens of other damnable atrocities – until journalist Seymour Hirsch startled the world with his discovery.

The villain is Lt. William Calley, commanding officer. But few remember the hero, pilot Hugh Thompson, who sees what is happening, lands his helicopter between our soldiers and the innocent victims, tells the troops to hold their fire, and if they don't, he and his two crew will open fire on them.

This is one righteous dude! He's lucky to have come out alive. Upon returning to *My Lai* thirty years later, villagers receive him with awe. Toward the end of the visit, one lady asks him, "But where are the perpetrators?" Following an awkward silence, she adds, "So we can forgive them." Wow!

Well, they didn't show up; they remained unforgiven.

May 25, 2020. Memorial Day

George Floyd, a black civilian, is brutally murdered on a street in Minneapolis by a racist cop and three accomplices – reckless, like sociopath

William Calley - officers of the law who regard themselves above the law with license to kill, sparking national and world-wide protests.

Suffocated by a knee on his neck, we have witnessed a modern-day lynching. George can barely utter the words *"I can't breathe"*. Consequently, the world is demanding systemic change in its criminal justice systems – while our divisive, white-supremacist President utilizes military force to disrupt peaceful protests, defying the Constitution and threatening public safety!

America's *original sin* is slavery. Southern churches proclaimed it as God's Will! In effect, being black was a crime. Black lives didn't matter, except as laborers, entertainers and playthings to grace the bedchambers of their masters. Following the Civil War, many Confederates swore "The South shall rise again!" They're still at it; the hatred is palpable – in this land called *"A City on a Hill"* (Boot Hill, it appears). And who's heard of the 1921 Tulsa, Oklahoma Race Massacre? Hardly a soul. School textbooks have been sanitized!

There was a protest song published in 1939, based on the lynching of a black man in Marion, Indiana in 1930, called *"Strange Fruit"* (made famous by Billie Holiday), which starts like this: *"Southern trees bear a strange fruit/Blood on the leaves and blood at the root/Black bodies swinging in the Southern breeze/Strange fruit hanging from the poplar trees...."*[12]

Protest songs like this gave rise to many more, and propelled people to active resistance against Jim Crow laws and segregation. Biblical prophetic imperatives, plus Enlightenment values, drove our black brothers and sisters to resist oppressive white imperialism.

Martin Luther King took a knee (1965) to pray, in Selma, Alabama. Colin Kapernick took a knee (2016) to protest police brutality and racial injustice, during the playing of the national anthem – as a gesture of respect

---

12   Abel Meeropol (1903-86) composed *"Strange Fruit"* in 1937, and published it in 1939 under the pen name "Lewis Allan". (James Baldwin was one of his high school students in New York).

for what the flag symbolizes: in particular, freedom of speech and *justice FOR ALL*. Soldiers take the knee facing the graves of fallen comrades. Today, conscientious cops are kneeling alongside protestors. *A knee can kill, or a knee can heal.*

The 1968 *Kerner Commission Report* concluded: *"Our nation is moving toward two societies, one black, one white – separate and unequal."* George Floyd's blood may prove to be the seed for a new society, more peaceful and just.

November 1970. Yucatan Peninsula, Mexico

Her name was Francisca. I say "was" because she is no longer with us. She was shot to death, a victim – like those at *My Lai*, and George Floyd – of brute violence.

Three years earlier, my student Gregorio (Francisca's and her husband Pablo's pastor) had established the village's first Protestant church, with a democratic, egalitarian ethos and zeal for charitable works – much to the chagrin of the village's four corrupt leaders.

After one of their drinking bouts, this lynch mob approaches Pablo's hut: "We accuse that scoundrel of peddling marijuana and stealing cattle! Where is he?"

Francisca is shocked. Never had her husband committed any such crimes. *His accusers did!* Pablo is in a nearby town, on horseback, purchasing something special for her birthday.

Jabbing a revolver into her ribs, they yell, "You're hiding him"; and unable to find him, they fire three shots. She slumps to the ground, her five little children standing by helplessly, in anguish, wailing.

Thinking her dead, these monsters issue an order: No one may approach the body – on pain of death. And to cover their tracks, they send a release to the Peninsula's morning paper stating they have eliminated an imminent threat to civil society.

Gregorio walks two hours from the nearest bus stop, approaches Francisca's house and finds her on the ground – but still breathing! Immediately, he sends boys to fetch a doctor and state authorities, and lets everyone know she's alive. He gently carries her to a hammock; she is quickly surrounded by seventy villagers, Christians and non-Christians alike, who stay with her 'til the moment she dies (twenty-four hours later).

Meanwhile, Pablo returns, present under his arm, but greeted by a doctor, state officials and scores of villagers. He sees the blood, his beloved racked with pain, and cannot contain himself; he is devastated. He then embraces her, while villagers weep.

Suddenly, she speaks with strength and clarity, telling her witnesses all that had happened, every detail from beginning to end. And as her hour approaches, gradually losing strength, she asks her sister, "Maria, will you take my five children and raise them as your own? Will you take Pablo as your husband?"

"Yes, Francisca, I will – with everything I am and have."

Thereupon, Francisca raises her arms as if beckoned by a higher power, her lips forming the word *"Vengo"* (I'm coming home).

The village tyrants were brought to justice, and most of the villagers became members of Francisca's church. Today, that village is a town; its inhabitants are thriving. Her blood became seed.

CHAPTER TWENTY-NINE.

THE BORDER

Mexico, 1971

It is my second year as Director, Yucatan Biblical Institute, Merida. I drive solo from Grand Rapids with gifts from supporting churches: Chevy *'Carry All' ('Suburban')*, washer, dryer, three air conditioners.

In our youth we were taught that God's elect have a divine invisible shield of protection. Believe me, you'll need it in Mexico. Cross the Rio Grande, all rights vanish, all freedoms evaporate. You're at their mercy: guilty until proven innocent. The world is topsy-turvy.

Bringing goods with you? Border agents will call them "contraband", then confiscate them or bribe you. No money? There's jail without bail (kidnap for ransom). Happens every day.

Agreed, we were warned: Mexico is one giant mafia, its bureaucracies riddled with crime. They'll frame, coerce and extort whomever they can. Border agents are paid little, but with enough bribes, they can retire in two years!

At the border, guards wave me through checkpoint one, then checkpoint two – enough to give one a sense of false security, "Hey, this is a breeze." Until checkpoint three, twenty miles inland – a barren wilderness (where no one can hear the screams of detainees). A guard hustles me out of the vehicle, seizes my keys and passport, and leads me to an interrogation room.

Their *modus operandi* is: intimidate, confiscate, incarcerate. They have it down to a science. Evil now stares me in the face. But I am resolute: 'Go ahead; do your worst; I won't budge' – as I quiver in my boots.

In a solitary moment, I breathe deeply, pray – and a soothing calm washes over me. I suddenly recall the role I played in our high school Senior Play *"Behind the Lines"*, a World War One spy drama, filled with intrigue, set in Gibraltar. In a flash, I know how to play this. *I've got to put on the dramatic performance of my life!*

But what, precisely, in this precarious predicament, will I say? What will I do? *It had better be convincing, or I'm toast!*

Survival instincts kick in: my family needs me; my school needs me; the villages need me (where government shows contempt for peasants). Moreover, my cause is just, because Mexican law allows residents on a tourist visa to take with them what they need if the products are for personal use only, and not for immediate resale. It's on the books. Not that any agent or hoodlum up the hierarchy cares!

As a guard prepares to drive my vehicle into the impound yard, he notices a flat back-right tire. *Something mysterious is happening.* I can feel it in my bones. Could a guardian angel be standing by me in this den of lions?

"Thank you, Lord," I whisper. "Now's the perfect opportunity!" Launching into my ruse, I declare (in Spanish): "Gentlemen, I am a good friend of the Minister of Tourism." I give them the exact name I had read in a leading newspaper. He made headlines arguing that a tourist-friendly Mexico will be a prosperous Mexico – an enterprise that must appear squeaky clean.

"Hear me, I'm a writer. I'm writing about Yucatan – which the world deserves to know more about. Your esteemed Minister has personally guaranteed my family a comfortable stay – therefore, this (not for resale) new car and appliances. But you can be certain of one thing: I will not pay you a single peso!" And following a pregnant pause, I hurl a challenge: "Go ahead, pick up the phone and ask him yourself!"

All four retreat to another room to discuss the matter. I can overhear them arguing about what to do – the pros and the cons. If what I claim turns out to be true, they can all lose their job, and therefore their income. Are they willing to take that risk?

I have them on the ropes, but the fight isn't over. Will they dare bribe me? Should they issue more than threats? But they're fully aware the more roughly they handle me, the greater the repercussions will be.

Not having reached a consensus, the matter still in limbo, they return to my room, "OK, Juanito, we're going to bring you outside and watch you change the tire."

I ask, "Could you please unlock the back, so we can get the spare?"

One of them reaches in and finally locates it - when, in a high-pitched voice I'll never forget, he lets out a scream "It's flat!!"

What?!?! *The force is with me.* Or as some Maya villagers would say, "It's the Jaguar's mystical power." *Beyond belief!* There are loads of things in life we cannot explain. In this case, both my captors and I stand dumbfounded.

Unforeseen, the entire mood changes. We all burst out laughing. None had ever seen the likes of this before. A consensus takes shape. Now they show empathy, commiserate. The leader exclaims, "This whole thing is jinxed. Let this guy go." No one objects. After all, everyone just witnessed a *bona fide* miracle.

They roll up their sleeves. "Juanito, you just sit over there, relax, and watch. We'll fix your tires and send you on your way." They hand me the keys and passport, a candy bar and a bottle of Coke, and bid me farewell, with fondest wishes.

No leaks all the way home. True story. Go figure! Still can't believe it. But it was not the first, or last, unusual event to have happened. There would be more to come.

CHAPTER THIRTY.

THE JUNGLE

Yucatan Peninsula, 1971

To enter the jungles of Yucatan is to enter the heart of darkness and leave behind the familiar. It's where the sidewalk ends.

The Maya were once astute astronomers and mathematicians, empire builders, masters of their universe. Their descendants in the hinterland, reduced to peasantry, seek mastery once more.

I assign my students field work in remote villages – places that Mexican social services ignore. Hopefully we will be perceived as midwives of progress, not as acquisitive 'ugly Americans'. It's all about mutual respect, dignity, collegiality.

My query is simple: "I'm here to listen. How can we help?"

Not everyone wants or needs help. Those who do, however, tend to show extraordinary hospitality. We eat primitive cuisine from a gourd with fingers, no fork. Special occasions call for pigs' head: "Eyes or brain, Juanito?" *Think fast!*

"No, jowl will do fine, thank you." Reminds me of the old missionary creed: *"Where he leads me I will follow; what they feed me I will swallow"*.

Accommodations: a typical oval-shaped stick-mud-thatched roof hut with openings on two sides, and hooks for hammocks. Drifting off to sleep, I hear things go bump in the night, and feel something brushing my bottom. Chickens, pigs and dogs amble in through one hut opening and out the other. "Not to worry, maestro, they're just part of the family". *'Free range', indeed!*

I don't know how these dear people get any sleep. It's noisier than New York City! My host exits the hut to pee behind a rock, and everybody's dogs begin barking. It never lets up; people keep getting up.

One evening, no longer able to bear all this turbulent traffic, this buttocks bumping and canine cacophony, I apologize to my host, and set out back to the main road, which lies several hours away. A few minutes out, it is dead quiet. Luckily, the weather is clear, and the moon is full.

Roads in the jungle are virtually nonexistent. You make do with paths and trails. The obstacles are endless. Rule number one: Never go out alone! That night, I am alone. I crawl ahead at a snail's pace. Watch out for those jagged rocks, those huge mounds of red ants, that monstrous iguana lumbering across the path!

And suddenly, at the stroke of midnight, like a thief in the night, two eyes in a huge, sleek muscular body materialize before my headlights. It can't be! It's something adventurers stalk as prey. Now, I'm the prey! Ambushed, I quake inside, and rush to roll up the windows. Have I been snared by the fangs of fate?

Resignation sets in: Reality courses through my veins: death is inevitable! If you gotta go, you gotta go. As good a way to go as any, I suppose. But something taps me on the shoulder and whispers: *No, doofus! Pull it together!*

A precocious predator, of course, loves the smell of fear. Its powerful paw can smash my window with one abrupt blow. I must make myself big! Take charge! Doesn't do any good being somebody's dinner.

My nocturnal nemesis slithers to the driver-side window. We lock eyes, only inches apart. It's a staring contest; time stands still. I'm in the presence of eternity. Its irises are gold: this is a god. What a night! Like a *burning bush* experience, but no voice. Like a face-to-face encounter with the real and mysterious Power of the Universe – in the form of a surrogate – the sacred Jaguar.

As the minutes pass, in this eternal void, the spell expires. And as if led by a higher essence, that elusive, solitary crusher of skulls is silently drawn back into the forest which it rules, and from which it came.

Awesome! Snatched once again from the clutches of oblivion! I reflect on this, after all these decades. What does it mean? I don't know. How do we determine this?

On a visceral level, the world is full of dangers (law of the jungle). And if you can't manage to save yourself, you may find yourself *being* saved again and again and again! So, have I been saved, again, *for* something? Perhaps. That always remains to be seen.

Rudolf Otto comes to mind – his 1917 masterpiece *Das Heilige (The Idea of the Holy)*. He says: The Divine is entirely beyond human comprehension. You can't define deity – in dogmas, creeds or confessions. Neither can you confine deity – in institutions or rituals.

However, you *can* experience the *"numinous"*, a profound feeling of *fear*, in two senses: *"mysterium tremendum"* - you're scared out of your wits; next, *"mysterium fascinans"* - you're awash in the wonder of a benevolent power which protects, nourishes and strengthens you.

Two stages: Shock and Awe!

"You mean, John, this is what happened to you in your face-to-face with the jaguar?"

"Absolutely."

"But it sounds a little subjective."

"Inevitably," I respond. "It reminds me of a *Peanuts* comic strip, with Lucy, Linus and Charlie Brown lying on their backs looking at the sky. Lucy says: 'You can see a lot of things in cloud formations. What do you see, Linus?' Linus replies, 'Well, over there I see a map of British Honduras. Over there I see a profile of Thomas Eakins, the famous painter. And over there I see the stoning of Stephen, with Paul standing nearby.' Lucy: 'And what do you see, Charlie Brown?' Charlie: 'Well, I was going to say a ducky and a horsie, but I changed my mind'".[13]

A New Age acolyte who hears my story comments: "Jaguars, John, are the coolest cats on the continent. Are you a Jaguar person? 'Jaguar People' are known to be 'honest, reliable, non-judgmental, non-controlling, and enthralled with the beauty and diversity of life.'"

"My goodness, all that?" I volley back. "If that's the case, perhaps we should all be more Maya. But my point in sharing this is: If you never feel vulnerable, you can never be courageous."

"Was it like a 'vision quest'?" she presses on.

"I wasn't looking for anything. It found me. The encounter was a stark reminder that death stalks us all. Life is fragile. But on both sides of the food chain, there's a will to live. On my side, it was an affirmation that I am loved, protected, empowered – for doing a little something in a little corner of the world that can make a little difference."

Isn't that about the most we can hope for on this planet – that our having been here will have made the world a little better place? And all these littles can add up to something really big. It takes a village. And that's not totally in our hands.

Such was my initial impression. A few weeks later, I am startled awake during a dream in which I encounter the Jaguar once more. It says: *"As I return to my forest, you must return to the land of your birth."* This is transformative. I see with new eyes. I will follow the dream.

---

13   Charles M. Schulz, in Robert L. Short, *The Gospel According to Peanuts* (Richmond, Virginia: John Knox Press, 1964), 33.

AMSTERDAM

1972–1975

CHAPTER THIRTY-ONE.

THE ZOO

A msterdam 1972-75
   "Nostalgia isn't what it used to be" (Peter De Vries), but here goes: While pursuing my mission in city and jungle, Professor G. C. Berkouwer (1903-96), the Netherlands' leading theologian, invites me to become his last doctoral student. (Very lucky! *Carpe diem!*) I am elated. Granted a sabbatical, we leave our Mexico mansion and come under his spell. His name means 'lumberjack'; he knows how to fell dead dogma and construct an ecumenical ship of hope. (He's not a *'yahoo'* – 'Yet Another Hierarchical Officious Oracle').

He's a master of active listening and effective dialogue, speaks not only so as to be understood, but also so as not to be misunderstood. *(No room for: "Weak argument, therefore shout!")* His knowledge is encyclopedic, his experience broad, his spirit conciliatory. It would be foolish not to absorb some of these exemplary traits – as my brother used to chide me: *"Be wise, not otherwise!"*

One big problem, however! Unlike Latin America, churches in Europe are dying – its buildings transformed into apartments and roller rinks, its congregations merging, simply to survive. This is an era of rapid change; everything is 'up for grabs'. The refreshing new orthodoxy of my mentor is already as good as dead!

Modern secularization, a process inaugurated by the eighteenth-century Enlightenment, is in full swing. But it's not a threat. It simply means that the functions once fulfilled by mother church have now been taken over by other institutions in society, her children. We're now cut loose from her apron strings.

I soon switch to Berkouwer's *protégé* and successor, Prof. Dr. H. M. Kuitert (1924-2017) as my mentor. This radical progressive thinker and media celebrity, tirelessly turning his world upside down, immediately has the Free University hire me as one of his research associates. He places my name beneath his on his office door. (Calvin Seminary professors there on sabbatical are shocked.) Is this real, or is this a dream? It's another incredible '*Forrest Gump* moment'.

Harry tells me: John, I had a tough time deciding between you and a fellow Dutchman. It was a toss-up. I chose you because your Uncle Willem, your dad's youngest brother, was my third-grade teacher in Drachten, Friesland. Your uncle brought out the very best in me, and already at that stage of life gave me a profound love of Dutch language and literature. He was my inspiration, my favorite teacher. How can I not choose you? Of course, you were also selected on your own merits. (Thanks for adding that!) Again, how mysterious. I had no idea my esteemed uncle, who mentored gifted students, had been his teacher.

My first assignment is to check out recent studies comparing human and non-human animal behavior (Ethology), and its implications for morality. (Nikolaas Tinbergen, Konrad Lorenz, Desmond Morris, Alexander Alland, E. O. Wilson....) We proceed scientifically 'from the bottom up', not from a supposed authoritative divine revelation 'from the top down'. Among the questions are: How much of our behavior is determined, and how much is 'free will'? Are human beings essentially 'good' by nature, or 'bad'? If we discount the myths of a Mohammed (Islam) or of a Joseph Smith (Mormonism), discovering absolute truth on buried golden tablets dropped from heaven - or, for that matter, the Christian Bible - then where do we get our norms and values for living?

It becomes clear to me that morality is a sphere totally independent of religion. In fact, it long preceded the advent of *homo sapiens*, with their inventions of gods and religions. What religions have done historically is pick-and-choose from the morality marketplace whatever suited their purposes. They simply placed their *'Good Housekeeping'* seal of approval on it (for example: slavery, women-as-chattel, greed-is-good, imperial expansion, rape of the environment), declaring it to be *'God's Will'!* This is still the way it works.

A visit to the zoo may help us sort things out. Zoos play a crucial role in helping humankind save us all (including all of nature) from ourselves. We're not far from extinction. Zoos promote stewardship, and help us recognize the interconnectedness of all life. In a pluriform world, we need norms, values and laws which keep tyrants and exploiters at bay. It is most enlightening to seek the roots of our moral behavior in the animal kingdom – of which we are only a small part.

Mythical religious schemes (such as *'Creation-Fall-Redemption'*, *'Original Sin'*, *'The Elect'*) have caused endless wars and misery. It's a miracle some good has come of it. To say that humans are born as essentially greedy and self-centered, plays into the hands of the Putins and Trumps of this world, of Wall Street, Dubai and Las Vegas. However, the belief 'born good' is also a delusion.

Most ethologists in the 1970s held that there is a huge cleft between humans and (non-human) animals: animals have *instincts* and are ruled by the 'law of the jungle', whereas, humans have developed *culture* (language, tools, rules, morality). If it did appear that animals showed human traits, such as love, loyalty or courage, it was regarded as no more than *anthropomorphism* – reading human behavior back into animal behavior.

Not so, says Dutch scholar Frans de Waal (Emory University, Atlanta, Georgia), my true hero in this field, who surfaces a decade later. His books are phenomenal. His hundreds of illustrations serve as cumulative evidence for his theory. Whereas, earlier evolutionary scientists focused on what drove human and non-human animals apart (competition, aggression), brilliant contrarian de Waal concentrates on what brings us together: reciprocity, empathy, conflict resolution – traits that are etched into our instincts, part of our DNA.

In a British zoo, a bonobo found a stunned bird lying in her enclosure. Says de Waal: "She picked it up, climbed the highest tree, unfolded the bird to (look like) a little toy airplane, and sent it out.... The bonobo put itself in the position of a totally different creature, an ability that we usually assume is uniquely human." (PBS: *"The Bonobo in All of Us"*, 2007)

Remarkable. Such sensitivities, abilities and actions have existed in animals tens of millions of years before we humans came along. Four million years ago, we were separated from our closest primate relatives, chimpanzees and bonobos. From them we inherited empathy, love and altruism – also the ability to feel pain, sadness, despair, ecstasy and joy.

It is true, male chimpanzees can be violent, killing rival males in a quest for females and territory; but they also find ways to resolve their conflicts, ending up hugging each other. Bonobos, a matriarchal and pacifist society, are the most empathetic. And this empathy was the first step in the evolution of morality. Once you live in groups, de Waal says, you have not only competition, but – in order to survive and thrive – you need tolerance and compassion as well.

So, are primates, including humans, born good, or evil? Studies show that we all, from the very beginning, possess both tendencies. A common Native American belief was: there are two creatures within each of us always struggling for supremacy: one good, and one evil. Which one wins? The answer: *Whichever one you feed!* This accords with de Waal's thesis and findings.

Add to this the sage advice of Abraham Lincoln: If you want it to go well with your soul, and with your world, then *"listen to the better angels of your nature"*, rather than the worse ones. We are the product of our choices.

Thirteenth-century Sufi poet Rumi ruminated he was a jackass with wings of angels. He chose to use his metaphorical wings. And presumably, they were of the better angelic variety.

When churches, religions, corporations, and politicians have failed us, we can again learn much from a focused study of nature, and keen observations at the zoo.

CHAPTER THIRTY-TWO.

THE UNDERDOGS

Amsterdam 1973

Today, June 8, 2018, is the ninetieth birthday of Peruvian Dominican priest Gustavo Gutierrez, father of *"Latin American Liberation Theology"* (yet another 1960s *'theology of the genitive case'*: Black Theology, Feminist Theology, Environmental Theology...*ad infinitum*). Theology is literally 'god-talk'. But all god-talk is projection (fantasy). All theology is, in reality, anthropology – human beings trying to make sense of their world and to figure out how they should live. For two thousand years, theology was philosophy baptized with god-talk. Since the 1960s, theology has become psychology, sociology, political science, biology, zoology and physics bathed in god-talk.

Why all this specialization? For some, it's a last-gasp measure to keep their dying academic discipline (theology) alive. For others, it's useful in shocking the world awake to gross systemic injustice, while goading church hierarchies to take action (giving churches a reason for continued existence).

Pope Francis, acknowledging his own past failures (in accord with passages like Jeremiah 2:34 "On your clothes is found the lifeblood of the innocent poor"), praises Father Gutierrez's "preferential option for the poor", which seeks to empower disenfranchised peasants, using techniques pioneered by Brazilian educator Paulo Freire (1921-97) in *Pedagogy of the Oppressed* (1968).

I immediately seize on this brand-new grass-roots movement in 1973. I digest Gutierrez's watershed book *A Theology of Liberation* (1973), in its context, and hustle to present my research (analysis and appraisal) in a special seminar for Dutch theological ethicists. Graduate students from *Apartheid*-fractured South Africa – whose lives upon returning home may be in mortal danger – participate. Steve Biko (1946-77) is one of their heroes (heavily influenced by Black intellectual Franz Fanon of Martinique, *The Wretched of the Earth*, 1963, and the Black Power movement in the U.S.) Within a few years Biko is assassinated by his racist government. (*Cry Freedom*, with Denzel Washington and Kevin Kline, 1987)

I find it curious, however, that never once does Father Gutierrez refer to fellow Dominican friar Bartolome de las Casas (1484-1566), who exposed Columbus and his compatriot Conquistadores as merchants of suffering and death. Las Casas' first-hand account states: "We came to serve God and get rich", but it soon becomes clear to him: *"Gold is their god"!* They massacred and enslaved millions of native inhabitants. Las Casas, in reaction, decides to become "Protector of the Indians", and proclaims to all: There is no salvation for you (Iberians) without social justice! "Christ did not come into this world to die for gold". *Las Casas blazed a trail for religious freedom and modern human rights.*

I was moved by the message and pathos of *The Mission* (1986), a portrayal of indigenous people two hundred years after Las Casas, victimized by landowners supported by the military and a corrupt church. Little had changed.

In an episode of *"The Young Indiana Jones Chronicles"* (masterpieces by George Lucas, 1992-93), an old man in Pueblo, Mexico, whose village was looted by Pancho Villa in 1916, laments (and I paraphrase): 'Years ago I rode with Benito Juarez against Emperor Maxmillian. I lost many chickens but thought it was worth it to be free. Then came Porfirio, Huerta, Carranza. They stole my chickens too. And now Pancho Villa!' These successive dictatorships did not differ much from the era of *The Mission* (mid-1700s). Clearly, Lucas echoes the great novel of the Mexican Revolution *Los de Abajo* (1915), *The Underdogs,* by Mariano Azuela (1873-1952).

Has the U.S. been 'exceptional'? No! says the *New York Times* of June 19, 2020: "Every form of oppression in the United States is based on stealing land, genocidal attacks on Indigenous people, and the enslavement of African-Americans."

Even the renowned Reformer Martin Luther (1483-1546), whose sayings are memorable – for example, *"I'd rather be ruled by a smart Turk (Muslim) than a stupid Christian"* - unfortunately had a dark side as well. He's a raving anti-Semite, unwittingly preparing the way for a Richard Wagner and Adolph Hitler. Wagner's musical genius is incontestable, but his ideology disastrous. Luther, moreover, sides with the German aristocracy to crush a massive Peasant Revolt (1524-25), resulting in widespread slaughter. He ignores Augustine's well-reasoned arguments against unjust war, written 1100 years earlier.

And Protestant Reformer John Calvin, though worshipped by many, has a dark side – ruling Geneva like an *Ayatollah*, executing political opponents such as Servetus! His entire theology supports his social system and political ends. Oscar Wilde was on target, famously stating: *"The only difference between the saint and the sinner is that every saint has a past and every sinner has a future."*

Where does the Bible come into all this? As *Resistance Literature.* "It brims with protest songs and prison letters, subversive poetry and politically-charged visions, satirical roasts of the powerful and storied celebrations of dissidents." (Rachel Held Evans, *Washington Post* July 12, 2018) Frequent Bible readings can turn you liberal, even radical (without having to be violent). Consider Dietrich Bonhoeffer (1906-45), Martin Luther King, Jr. (1929-68), even Orlando Costas (1942-87).

Orlando and I, with our families, were next door neighbors in Costa Rica (1970) and close neighbors in The Netherlands (1974). Orlando was an unstoppable force of nature, having converted large numbers of Latin Americans to Protestantism. We are in constant dialogue as he writes his dissertation at the Free University. He increasingly immerses himself in Liberation Theology, becoming a passionate voice for justice and peace in society.

Born in Puerto Rico to Methodist parents, Orlando's family takes up residence in New York City when he is twelve. The uprooting is traumatic. He is immediately confronted with ridicule, prejudice, racism, hostility, and is quickly caught up in territorial gang fights. The sweet kid becomes an angry young man. But he is also reflective: Why does life have to be this way? How can we change it? So, Orlando experiences three conversions.

1) His first conversion takes place at a Billy Graham Crusade – his *Fundamentalist* (saved-soul) phase. He goes directly to Bob Jones University, in South Carolina. But he is met there with virulent racism, an extremely legalistic value system, plus a triumphalistic belief in the divine *Manifest Destiny* of the United States!

2) His second conversion is to his Latin American identity, rejecting American economic colonialism, and taking up the cause of struggling minorities – via community activism (like young Barack Obama in South Chicago). This is his *Liberal* phase.

3) His third conversion is his *Prophetic* phase – called to confront the destructive powers-that-be with a 'spirituality for combat', putting his life on the line. He wrote many books, informed by careful research and personal experience, the most influential being *Christ Outside the Gate* (1982): if you really want to meet the Christ, the place you'll find him is in the outcast, the needy, the marginalized – outside your comfort zone. Reach out, bear their suffering. Tall order!

Orlando moves on to leadership in progressive U.S. seminaries, plus involvement in Catholic and Protestant ecumenical organizations. He pours himself into the lives of others and brings out the best in everyone he meets, before burning out at the age of forty-five.

Liberation of the oppressed is always from something and for something – in the most general terms: from death to life, from despair to hope. But in the process, life goes on – there are birthdays, weddings, and a barrel of things to celebrate. So let there be singing, dancing, joy and humor! It's exhilarating to hear good laughter. Liberation produces laughter, and laughter is liberating.

MINNEAPOLIS

1975–1982

CHAPTER THIRTY-THREE.

ALTERNATE UNIVERSE

M*inneapolis 1975*
        In Holland, amid the recession and layoffs caused by the OPEC oil embargo (October 1973 - March 1974), I'm uneasy. The last ones hired in the Dutch university system are the first ones fired. But when the axe falls at year's end, we're in luck! An invitation wings its way from First Christian Reformed Church, Minneapolis, to be their pastor. It becomes our home from 1975 to 1982.

However, we experience culture shock upon returning to the States, because we enter an alternate ecclesiastical universe. The preceding three years in the Netherlands were intellectually liberating – my *'Damascus Road'*. We tackled big issues, like *Apartheid*, gender equality, animal rights – all of which were taken up by Dutch politicians and converted into legislation. Heady stuff! Thought led to action.

But now we are greeted by narrow concerns for one's own soul – *Me-ism*. One family, as unassailable proof of their personal piety, guides me into their private prayer room. "Those indentations in the carpet were made by our knees," they boast. *I've already seen enough!*

This spiritual solipsism, I discover, is a nationwide problem. It feels like a frontal attack. Fundamentalism (the Bible as 'Paper Pope', cast into rigid literalistic molds) and Perfectionism (certain Weslyans and holy-roller Charismatics) are in the process of invading mainline churches

(Lutheran, Methodist, Presbyterian, Reformed, Baptist, Congregational, Episcopalian), attempting to subvert existing authority and practice – much like attempted *coups* by certain Gnostics in early Christianity.

First CRC is not immune to this onslaught. One third of our congregation are traditionalists *("Faith of our Fathers, holy faith…").* Another third are progressive, university-educated professionals. A final third are less educated and easily swept away by every current. This last group is vocal and demanding. They are the new *Chosen*; they are *in*; all others are *out*.

What brought this about? Especially Bill Gothard. He herded millions of church people into urban arenas, where he mesmerizes both young and old, through visuals and a soft delivery. His one-man, multi-day *Institute in Basic Youth Conflicts* is always sold out. He presents easy steps to solve every personal and family problem.

It's pure legalism: "Just follow my list of rules, and you'll be less conflicted, more fulfilled, happier and holier" – far beyond the struggling peons you leave in your wake. ('Peon' literally means: 'Pee on', connoting a rank lower than 'Untouchable'). He backs every step and every rule with proof texts and illustrations from Old and New Testaments.

"Everything you'll ever need is right here in the Bible," he says. "You just haven't found it yet – until now. Follow my prescriptions, and you'll become persons of stellar character – unblemished by the world. Do home schooling, and become the new leaders of church and government."

Very few today know Gothard's name – the person who was embraced by Mike Huckabee, Sarah Palin and the Reality TV Duggan family! He preferred to remain low key, behind the scenes, the leaven that quietly gives rise to holy bread. Almost single-handedly he accelerated the decline of mainline churches in America, while propping up Fundy fanaticism – the Religious Right and its 'Moral Majority'.

But in 2014, as with his televangelist counterparts, the oversight Board he himself had created forced him to step down, after decades-long allegations of sexual harassment and molestation. His behavior had come to exhibit the characteristics of *an authoritarian cult guru, in which the leader believes he's above his own rules for everybody else.* History is littered with such folly.

At times I'd humor our church's bible-thumpers, by echoing their *guru*, Gothard. When asked whether one should tithe based on gross income, or net income, I mimic the answer: "Well, think about it – do you want God to bless the gross, or the net?" After their concurrence, with audible chuckles, I add: "Literalistic tithing is nonsense, of course. Wherever your highest value lies, you'll give it all you've got – not a percentage!"

I ask my amiable Conservative Jewish dentist about this. We've built a good relationship, and he finally accepts our invitation to lunch at the parsonage – after being convinced the meal would be kosher. As to tithing, he says: "No, we don't take that literally. All we need from each family is two percent. That's enough to cover the entire synagogue budget, including our private school."

"Wow, that's incredible! But how do you know every family's financial worth and income? How do you know they're not cheating?"

"Believe me, we know."

CHAPTER THIRTY-FOUR.

BRUBAKER

First CRC Minneapolis has a diverse membership, representing almost every field of endeavor. Students and faculty from the University of Minnesota (math, physics, psychology, medicine, music, philosophy) are also attracted to our worship services.

There's one person who frequently slips into a back pew after the service begins, and disappears abruptly when it ends. I catch up with him a few times (1975-79), finding his story most intriguing. It turns out he's U of M Professor of Law Thomas Murton.

Tom is a leading advocate of US prison reform – more humane treatment of inmates, safer environment, opportunities for personal growth, combating abuse and corruption. Beginning in 1959, he helped the new State of Alaska establish its penal system.

In 1967, Governor Winthrop Rockefeller hires Murton as Arkansas' first professional penologist. Little by little, as Warden of Cummins State Prison, he hears stories from prisoners of the torture, murder and disappearance of past and fellow inmates. Sure enough, he discovers bodies buried on prison grounds!

The Governor wants the atrocities covered up. "No way," says Tom. Rockefeller fires him! The story is told in his 1969 book: *Accomplice to Crime: The Arkansas Prison Scandal...of 1967*. Twentieth Century Studios released *Brubaker* in 1980, starring Robert Redford, dramatizing Tom's experience. In the time I knew him, these events stirred strong emotions in him, insomnia as well.

Having met Professor Thomas Murton, I volunteer my pastoral services at Stillwater State Prison, a raucous place, always on the brink of chaos. As the metal doors clang shut behind me, it feels like Dante's *Inferno: "Abandon hope all ye who enter here"!* Glad I'm not here when the bloody riots break out.

My experience is akin to the Head Chaplain's description: Inmates all claim they're innocent. They "come to Jesus" to have their sentences reduced. They're consummate con artists. Recidivism rates are high. I do, however, glimpse moments of true humanity, and have a persistent gut feeling that while many do not belong here, several on the outside do.

In our Minneapolis church, the majority of congregants are Republicans, a quasi-religion superseding Calvinism or ecumenism. I do not cater to them, even though some demand pulpit reinforcement. Solution? A project that will pull us together. In 1975 I hear that the State Department is working closely with Lutheran World Relief to resettle Vietnamese refugees in the U.S. I want us to be at the top of their list to sponsor families. Our deacons, in turn, manage to enlist the resources and enthusiasm of the entire congregation. We're off to a good start. We help our first refugee family with housing and employment – no strings attached. We're here to help you, not convert you. We sponsor twelve more families in rapid succession. This is one of many things everyone could get behind. But, mess with their politics – expect fireworks!

CRC people call me from all over the country: Could you please visit my relative at the Mayo Clinic-affiliated St. Mary's Hospital in Rochester? "Glad to do so." Also, the University of Minnesota Hospital in St. Paul. A young man with scoliosis from Grand Rapids, Michigan, is there, suspended upside down in a Jungle Jim-like contraption (inversion therapy). I get down on all fours, introduce myself, and decide to lay flat on my back facing him looking down at me. His cheeks are red. Good banter, of course: "How's it hangin', Dude?" Upon departure: "Hang in there"! *He needs a friend. He has one in me for a while.*

Years later, when my dad passed away in Grand Rapids, this same young man – now walking erect - comes to see me at the wake. He says, "I read the obituary in the *Press* and I knew I had to come. You were there for me in Minnesota. Now I want to be here for you." I am deeply moved. It reminds me of Luke 17:17, where only one out of many who were healed show up to give thanks, expressing solidarity and hope. He too is such a rare gem.

In 1982, a parishioner tells me she is about to star, unwittingly, in a forthcoming novel by Alistair MacLean, to be called *Floodgate*. It would be one of his last before he dies in 1987. Dan Brown, decades later, is more exciting - all action and cliffhangers, but MacLean is good - no gratuitous sex or violence, yet lots of intrigue.

In *Floodgate* (1983), international terrorists threaten to destroy the Netherlands by blowing its main dikes to smithereens. MacLean, a Scot, had spent a good deal of time in Holland. In real life he is the friend of a wealthy, successful industrialist named Jaap, who later discovers that he and his daughter Thea have been morphed into two of the main characters of his novel. Ever after, I could visualize my former parishioner in no way other than a mythical heroine!

On a lighter note, I take our oldest son, active in Youth Orchestra, to hear Leonard Slatkin conduct the Minnesota Orchestra. We're in the front row, taking it all in. Afterward, we sweet talk our way into the Green Room to meet the performers. Slatkin to our son: "Young man, is this your first time at Orchestra Hall?" – to which he replies, "No sir, I've played here!" Slatkin is at a loss for words, managing a weak grin. We return home with his autograph and smiles on our faces.

CHAPTER THIRTY-FIVE.

MINNESOTA MIRACLE

M*inneapolis 1980*
Wendell Anderson (1933-2016) was a luminary in the
Democratic Party, tight with Hubert Humphrey and Walter Mondale – a
true presidential hopeful. He's humble, charismatic, athletic (1956 Winter
Olympics Silver Medalist in Hockey), intelligent, articulate, indefatigable.
Elected Governor in 1970 at age 37 (serving 1971-76), he reaches across
party lines, and demonstrates to the nation that working together beats
hanging alone.

Anderson's bipartisan *"Minnesota Miracle"* places him on the August
13, 1973 cover of *Time* magazine. Six years of progressive legislation earns
him the accolade *"Midwestern Kennedy"*.

But then comes a sudden reversal of fortune, his fall from political
grace and flight into the shadows. When Walter Mondale gives up his
Senate seat to become Vice President under Jimmy Carter, Anderson
decides to engineer his own appointment to Mondale's vacant seat. The
electorate takes exception to this self-ordination, and decisively votes him
and much of the DFL (Democratic-Farmer-Labor Party) out of office.

In yet another incredible succession of *'Gump* events', it turns out we
are members of the same health club and maintain a similar schedule. After
workouts, we relax in the spa (about six people). Wendy is reconciled to his
fate. None of us ever brings up the subject. We talk about sports (Vikings,

Twins, North Stars, University of Minnesota teams), about business and trade, social ideals and values, what our churches are doing for our community.... He's proud of his accomplishments, but not self-congratulatory. "I was privileged to be governor when people were nice to one another. Republicans and Democrats got along.... They respected one another." *(New York Times,* July 18, 2016) Quite a contrast to our current (2017) polarization pandemic! There's something to be learned here.

Inspired by Wendy, I decide to pick up the political torch in my own modest way when Ronald Reagan with George H.W. Bush is campaigning against incumbent President Jimmy Carter with Walter Mondale in 1980. I am incensed about Reagan's support of extreme right-wing oppressive dictatorships in Latin America (heavily influenced by ideologist Jeanne Kirkpatrick).

Having lived and worked in Latin America, and having researched, written about and conducted seminars in the Netherlands on the new phenomenon called "Latin American Liberation Theology", I cannot be silent.

Amnesty International produced detailed reports on U.S. corporations that, by way of U.S. government-sponsored goons (proxies), "disappeared" (covertly imprisoned, tortured and murdered) activists and organizers of trade unions in Central America. Unions were a threat to cheap labor, and cut into big corporations' bottom lines.

Archbishop Oscar Romero, targeted by the Salvadoran government for his solidarity with activists and victims of torture, and for his public denunciations of extrajudicial murders, was assassinated at the altar while saying mass. He has been canonized as both Martyr and Saint by the Roman Catholic Church. (Read Joan Didion's essay, describing her own "terrifying" experience: *Salvador,* 1983).

So, I join with dozens of protesters, marching and doing sit-ins at the Federal Building. People of diverse religious and political persuasions participate – liberal evangelical activists *(Sojourners),* pacifists, socialists, relatives of the "disappeared". Organize a demonstration, and it never fails: the media show up – fastest way to get the word out. I am one of the protesters they decide to interview. Next day, my name is in the newspaper. Rumblings ensue: "Guess what our pastor's been up to!"

I have no choice. The following Sunday morning, I stand behind the pulpit of First CRC Minneapolis, deciding to get ahead of the controversy, and declare: "Brothers and Sisters, by now you've probably heard about your pastor's foray into the political arena. My opinions are strong, born of experience. But they are my personal views as a private American citizen doing his civic duty. By no means do I speak for you, for this congregation, or for our denomination. In fact, I encourage you to do the same. Whatever your position, get involved; let your voices be heard. Thank God for freedom and democracy, which makes this possible." That stated, the worship service commences.

With the new Administration installed in Washington DC, what happens is exactly what had been predicted: support for extreme right-wing dictators, resulting in Reagan's infamous "Iran-Contra Scandal", arms-for-hostages, with no one ultimately held accountable!

Given my sudden notoriety, mainline church pastors get together and announce, "John, you wild-eyed radical (obvious hyperbole), we've elected you President of the Edina Ministerial Association." That's what happens when you become vocal! Two exciting years follow. We even prayed for the Minnesota Vikings, but that didn't help any!

In a lighter vein, I receive a letter from Petro, a fellow pastor in the Netherlands. He's good with young people – rescues kids from the streets, and helps them discover a purpose for living. He writes, "John, old buddy, I formed a Christian rock band and male/female chorus, twenty strong. We've toured Europe. Now we're doing the U.S. Want us to perform in Minneapolis? Just provide food, lodging, a venue, and take an offering to cover travel. We each have a sleeping bag. Perhaps we can crash on your pews."

The church council approves, with one caveat: "Separate the girls from the boys at night. They mustn't get ideas! Females stay with families; males snooze in the pews." Unlike their sheltered 'new world' counterparts, these budding European youths – with the advent of modern condoms – are accustomed to mingling indiscriminately.

The evening performance is well-received and packed to overflowing. Biggest draw they ever had. Under silent protest, they accept our condition of nocturnal chastity. Next morning, the Ladies' Society, busy preparing a hot breakfast in the church kitchen, is struck dumb, blushing every shade of red – that is, before giddiness sets in. Why? Because at *reveille,* the guys jump out of their sack butt-naked, do a slow streak through the kitchen-dining hall *en route* to the bathroom, with pious onlookers' mouths agape. A veritable nude review - in the house of God – from wee little Willy to pistol Pete. Ladies, "*Smakelijk eten* (Dutch), *Bon Appetit*, Enjoy"!

Last night, they're rockin'. At dawn's early light, they're rollin'. Never in the history of this congregation had anyone been treated to such a dramatic encore. *The running of the bulls, indeed.*

CHAPTER THIRTY-SIX.

GOAL!

January 17, 1981

Never did I imagine I'd stand on center ice before seventeen thousand screaming fans! But it happened.

We attended countless North Star games, especially when young Wayne Gretzky, "The Great One", came to town. This season, there's a drawing to enter a Shootout contest (prize: a new Ford). And would you believe? My name is drawn! Select season games feature a Shootout with three contestants. Winners of each will face off in a final match.

I have six weeks to practice before my scheduled debut. Fortunately, there are ice rinks in almost every public park, maintained by area cities for three full months. So into the frigid outdoors I venture, with my sons, to figure out a foolproof way to hold the stick and control the direction and speed of the puck.

In this contest, you have to stand at a designated spot between the red line and blue line, select a hockey stick (left-handed or right-handed), then shoot the puck down the ice through a narrow slot in a piece of plywood placed in front of the goal net. Very tricky. High degree of difficulty.

One day, I find the answer. "Eureka!" I've got this: I'll place my left hand down on the neck of the stick, near the blade. Instead of taking a big swing, which everyone tends to do, I'll direct the puck through that elusive opening with a short forward movement and sudden, explosive force.

Okay, I admit it looks unorthodox – my butt high in the air. But so what? *Let 'em laugh. I'm gonna win!* We'll see who laughs last.

Free tickets arrive for the whole family – best seats in the house. We tell no one about this event, to minimize the embarrassment – as in, what's our preacher doing in this circus? The game itself is thrilling. Minnesota Center Bobby Smith scores three goals (a 'hat trick'), in a game which helps propel them to the Stanley Cup Finals.

The First Period ends and, before the Zamboni arrives to sweep and resurface the rink, we three contestants make our way to the ice. I'm shaking in my boots. It's a big gig, seventeen thousand fans watching every nuance – merciless to losers, passionate about winners. I'm third in line.

The first to be called is a young woman – allowed two shots to score one goal. She steps up, selects a stick, swings – and the puck swerves way to the left. The fans are cruel; they boo and hiss. Again she swings; it curves right; spectators are uncivil, expressing scorn. I feel her pain; tears trickle from her dark brown eyes. Why can't they just applaud her for trying?

A middle-aged male steps up. Both pucks hit the plywood; the crowd's jeering is infelicitous.

Finally, my name is announced. I step forward nervously, knowing how vicious the masses can be. I take a deep breath, rehearse the moves in my mind, get into position, leaning way down – with my keister (as Reagan calls it) aimed up and at the audience. Fans explode with laughter. 'He looks so unconventional, so ridiculous.'

Whereupon, I tap the puck with proper force and direction, and – *Voila!* Fireworks! – at once, the fickle crowd erupts not with jeers, but cheers! The reverberations are deafening. The puck went in! Into the net! Unbelievable. I throw my arms into the air, stick and all, like Wayne Gretzky, in a big V for victory.

The person in charge asks me: "Wanna go again? You're already in the finals, but you're entitled to two shots. See if you can do it again."

I'm pumped. "Sure, I'm game. Watch me do it again" I assume my familiar eccentric pose. *No laughter this time, only silence,* eager anticipation. You can hear the proverbial pin drop. I concentrate, step up, tap the puck with measured oomph – and the arena goes wild! Again I throw my arms into the air like Gretzky in a V for victory amid thunderous fleeting acclaim. I make the ascent to rejoin my family, receiving pats on the back, with "Way to go, lefty!"

Beyond belief: Smith scored three that night in a 7-1 victory over Quebec, and I scored two! Well, it wasn't over yet. Next day, after the morning church service, I was swarmed by young people: "PAS-tor JO-hn! We couldn't believe our eyes. That was YOU out there in the middle of the rink." They now see their preacher in an entirely different light.

I respond: "Glad you loved it – as I've been saying, 'All things are possible.'"

March 12, 1988

A shy young boy named Chad, age nine, must have been somewhat impressed by his pastor's debut on North Star ice January 17, 1981. This boy went on to glory. I don't mean he died. I mean he felt he had died and gone to heaven on a very special day in his life.

We had moved to California in 1982. One day, March 12, 1988, tuning in by chance to ESPN, a hockey game caught my attention - final game of the Minnesota High School State Championships. Lo and behold, there was Chad, sophomore age sixteen, playing Center for Edina High School. What an athlete! What a game! A matchup to remember! (Check it out on *YouTube*) At the very end of the contest, Chad broke loose, flew toward the net like "Rocket Richard" – every kid's dream of glory – made a sweet move, faked out the goalie, and punched in his celebrated goal. Goal number five was the frosting on the cake and gave Edina its eighth coveted championship. Who would have thought! Shy in his youth like New Testament Timothy, he emerged as bold, energetic and victorious.

LOS ANGELES

1982–

CHAPTER THIRTY-SEVEN.

QUESTION ALL ANSWERS

Calvin College 1962

The new Knollcrest Campus of Calvin College beckons in 1962. Ours is the inaugural freshman class. The Library-Classroom Building, by some inexplicable coincidence, has the exact dimensions of Noah's mythical Ark. So, we call it *"The Ark"*. Ironically, soon after opening, it rains so hard, the basement floods! *The denominational lifeboat isn't leak proof after all.*

On the shuttle bus between the old Franklin Street campus and the Ark, I meet the most fascinating individuals. One is a Cuban refugee seminarian, converted from our mother Roman Catholic Church. He relates hilarious stories about his roommate at the Catholic University of Havana – who never studied (he did other things, you might say), crammed a couple of nights before major exams and aced them all, preferring to do things his own way. His name? Who would have guessed? Fidel Castro!

A couple of years later, I meet a new person on the bus – Johannes, a middle aged Canadian Dutch immigrant who feels called to be a preacher. I help him with ancient Greek. At his family dinner table he prays for Hank, their wild-child. Sure enough, Hank does a 180, turning toward the other extreme. He takes over a radio show called *"The Bible Answer Man"*. Pompous title! It suggests: My interpretation of 'God's infallible truth' represents authentic 'historic Christianity'. Better, I would suggest, is the scientific approach: Question all answers! He has accomplished some good, however – exposing modern cults: what they believe, and how they operate. Sadly, he ignores how cultic he himself has become.

Minneapolis 1979

In 1979, during one of my frequent trips to the Netherlands, I look up Johannes at his parsonage in a small town east of Rotterdam. He says I'm a godsend. After four years in that place, he wants out, but has nowhere to go.

"What's causing the flak?" I inquire.

"They want women in ecclesiastical office; and I don't," he responds.

"Johannes, obviously you're in the wrong place, at the wrong time. I'll help you if I can. But you do realize the awkward truth that we're at opposite ends of the stick on this issue! I've championed the full equality of women in every regard for as long as I can remember."

I ask myself: *"Am I my brother's keeper?"* even if we disagree on major issues? Of course I am. That's what we're called to be. So I scroll through my mind: He shows pastoral compassion. He's on a Dutch radio station nightly, signing off with a devotional. So far, so good. Then it dawns on me that he'd be a perfect fit for a vacant pulpit in Canada, a member of our international Classis Minnesota North. "Johannes, how would you and your wife like to move to Winnipeg, Manitoba? Most parishioners are immigrants, speak Dutch, don't want women in office – perfect match. But let me ask you one favor in return: Please don't become overly-defensive on the gender issue! You know change will come; it's only a matter of time."

"Fair enough," he replies, desperate to get out of there.

"So, shall I put in a good word for you?"

"Absolutely."

"Okay, you may very well have an official call on your desk within two months" – which is exactly what happened, and they moved to Winnipeg post haste. (Sadly, however, he did keep pushing his women-as-second-class agenda!)

Los Angeles 1984

We move from Minneapolis to Los Angeles in 1982 to pastor an aging congregation of Dutch immigrants, refreshingly tolerant in outlook. They want me to help them close down operations within four years. After that, I'm going into business.

I decide to contact Joan, a former classmate, who is spearheading something she calls "CW-CRC" ("Committee for Women in the CRC"). I ask: "Joan, could you coordinate a day of lectures and workshops on 'women in ecclesiastical office' at our Rehoboth Church? No other congregation of ours in California is willing to take this on!

"I'm in," she says, "great opportunity."

We get the word out, and on February 4, 1984, our auditorium is filled to capacity! Most participants are college educated professionals. The CRC Synod, predictably, keeps putting off the issue at hand (way behind the parade, as usual), by appointing one study committee after another.

Joan choses excellent presenters, sustains attendees' interest, and has me speak on "those sticky verses", like "women shall remain silent…." No big deal; my voice joins thousands of others, demonstrating how such words have been misinterpreted for two thousand years.

That done, I am asked to say a brief prayer before lunch. I pray: "Dear Father/Mother in heaven…", and hear an audible gasp from someone in back of the auditorium. After (almost) everyone returns home enthused, Joan says: "John, some people just aren't ready for that yet."

"Well, here I come - ready or not! God has a gender? Isn't the Deity depicted in Scripture both fatherly and motherly, tough and tender?" I add, "To make progress, you can't be that thin-skinned. After all, we're not advocating the Catholic idea of Mary '*Theotikos*' ('Mother of God'), nor are we resurrecting a primitive pagan Mother Goddess." I conclude: "Let's not deny the obvious – *assuming, of course, that a God truly exists who corresponds to our notions.*"

My mother breast-fed me with belief in the full equality, dignity and worth of all God's children. I took that for granted as the natural order of things. She said: "Someday, John, perhaps you can do something to help advance the cause of equality." It stuck with me. I regarded as aberrational those who advocate or practice inequality.

When churches must learn again from secular society what is good, just and humane, it indicates they are behind the curve, have lost their mandate to be 'salt and light', and have – to that extent – become quite expendable.

CHAPTER THIRTY-EIGHT.

JESUS LAND

M*id-1980s*
          Julia Scheeres came out with her gripping memoir *Jesus Land*
in 2005. I discovered it by chance in 2018. It swept me away! Couldn't put it
down. Gifted writer! Compelling true story. (*New York Times* Best Seller).
The events transpire during the mid-1980s, while I am shepherding my
last congregation, in California.

The white writer, born 1967, has two adopted black brothers. They're
members (small world!) of the Lafayette (Indiana) Christian Reformed
Church. Her father, a surgeon, is a violent, abusive disciplinarian. Her
mother, a nurse, is numbingly distant and hypercritical – more concerned
with missions and church societies than with her own children!

Public high school is hell for them – endless abuse from redneck
students. To make matters worse, their dysfunctional Calvinist parents
send Julia and David (same grade, same age – Julia always protective of
her brother) to Escuela Caribe in the Dominican Republic – which turns
out to be a harsh fundamentalist, cultic Christofascist concentration camp.
They survive all this. Then David, sadly, dies in an auto accident at age 20.

At heart, the memoir is a brother-sister love story. In and through all
the racism, they are there for each other. It's a story that tugs at the heart-
strings – makes you sad, mad and glad. In the end, Julia declares, "I can no

longer have blind faith in creeds, because I am no longer blind."[14] Brutally honest, liberating, therapeutic.

Having completed the reading, I do a little online research. I discover that Rev. Gordon Blossom, founder of Escuela Caribe, first established "New Horizons Youth Ministries" in Lowell and Grand Rapids, Michigan in 1971 – providing a 'home' for young people from dysfunctional families. But as a result of abusive treatment of his charges, Blossom loses his foster license in Michigan, and moves to Indiana (no regulations!). In Marion, Indiana, judges send him wards of the State for tough-love rehabilitation; and big bucks begin flowing into his coffers. *(Ka-ching!)*

Thereupon, he sets up shop in an obscure region of the Dominican Republic – a 'Christian' military-style camp for 'troubled youth', licensed by the State of Indiana Department of Child Services. *Megabucks!* He also begins advertising in Christian magazines (*Christianity Today*): Send us your problem kids; we'll straighten them out ($4,000 per child, per month. *Ka-ching!*).

However, they are not, in fact, being monitored by the State; little education takes place; and young people emerge from that hell-hole with PTSD. Several commit suicide. Moreover, in 1991, it was discovered that the entrepreneurial, violent, sex-addicted Rev. Blossom had for years abused his own family and solicited sex from young third-world (preferably virgin) prostitutes!

Scheeres' second book (*A Thousand Lives*, 2011) is about another Blossom-like cultic preacher, originally from Indiana, Rev. Jim Jones – who deceived, abused, and eventually - by forced mass suicide – murdered over 900 of his captive followers in Jonestown, Guyana, South America. Ms. Scheeres draws many parallels to Escuela Caribe.

Upon further reading (just take it where it leads), here's the real kicker: In 2011, all of Blossom's operations are shut down. His license is revoked by the Department of Child Services, State of Indiana. What happens? The

---

14   Julia Scheeres, *Jesus Land* (New York: Counterpoint, 2005), 354.

enterprise immediately reopens under a different name, while retaining the same staff for the next five years! Fort Wayne-based Lifeline Youth and Family Services creates a subsidiary, Crosswinds, to take over Escuela Caribe and renames it Caribbean Mountain Academy. They add 'Gay Conversion Therapy' to their list of offerings!

Some parents hire professionals to kidnap their gay son or daughter, and forcibly deliver them there! The "school" starts charging families up to $6,000 per month, per student. *(Ka-ching!)* They deliberately conceal their history, and launch a new marketing blitz. 'Teen brokenness' has become *a lucrative multi-billion-dollar industry*!

To top it off: Mike Pence, Governor of Indiana (2013-17) is a close friend of Lifeline founders and leaders, facilitating a flow of taxpayer revenue to their business. They are very much 'in bed together'. In 2012, he had made a Lifeline official a director of his gubernatorial campaign! Reciprocal loyalty. Something fishy going on here?

The Democratic candidate that Pence very narrowly defeated? John R. Gregg, my step-father-in-law Lary's (town judge of Demotte) close friend and cousin. (How would things be different if Gregg had won? One can only speculate!)

Pulitzer Prize winning conservative columnist George F. Will excoriates Pence as "the worst person in government", *Washington Post*, May 9, 2018. The descriptor which sends us all to the dictionary is *"oleaginous"*. Pence is 'oily, greasy' – too smooth for comfort, perversely ingratiating, fawning, flattering. We could add: lack of integrity, servile, sycophant, lackey, groveler, self-seeker, *echolaliac* (slavishly repeats and reinforces every foolish thing Trump says). Mr. Will concludes with these words: "Trump is what he is, a floundering, inarticulate jumble of gnawing insecurities and…vanities, which is pathetic. Pence is what he has chosen to be, which is horrifying."

Yet another online surprise: I look up "Lafayette CRC". There are two churches. The newest is "Sunrise CRC" – embroiled in a huge recent scandal. Its pastor was caught in April 2012 for having installed hidden video cameras in the women's restrooms of the church - disguised as air fresheners! He was eventually sentenced to four years in Indiana State Prison. Upon release, he'll be 62; he'll then serve three years probation, and enjoy 'adult sex offender' status for the rest of his life.

Amazing what you bump into while doing a little surfing online.

CHAPTER THIRTY-NINE.

WOW!

It's *1986*. I've resigned honorably from my pastoral duties in the CRC, and am about to spread my entrepreneurial wings, when – as if preordained – I meet the right person at the right time!

I had attended business lunches at the Crystal Cathedral for several years. Rev. Dr. Herman (Bud) Ridder walks over and introduces himself. He's the new second-in-command at the Cathedral, rescuing Robert Schuller from yet another imminent bankruptcy. You've got to be kidding! – Bud and his wife have been good friends of my parents-in-law for decades – and I reveal my relationship. Instantly, it's as if we've known each other for years.

"John, join us at the Cathedral. We can use your talents. Membership is transitory – easy come, easy go." Without delay, I teach a class and lead a retreat, my wife sings in the *"Hour of Power"* Choir, our kids perform in the *"Glory of Christmas"* pageant and the *"Hour of Power"* Orchestra.

Visiting Bud on campus midweek, Bob Schuller strolls toward us, with a huge scroll tucked under his arm. Bud exclaims: "Bob, I want you to meet my good friends, John and Cheri, new members…." That's all it takes to make us Bob's new best friends – *for the moment*. Bud exits.

And for the next twenty minutes, non-stop, with the excitement of a kid in a candy shop, Bob says: "Look at this," unfurling his blueprints. "You're the very first ones, after me, to see them. Just received them. Know what it is?" he asks teasingly. *No idea.* "It's going to be built right here where you're standing, on this very spot (next to the glass Cathedral). It'll reach up to, but no higher than, the arms of the cross atop our fourteen-story office building. It'll have a prayer chapel below, with carillons playing above. It will be the most beautiful bell tower anywhere on earth! Every cathedral needs one." This is Schuller's appeal: People love feeling they're a part of something much bigger than themselves.

Some of us jokingly referred to Bob as the "Bishop of Garden Grove", since if this were a *bona fide* cathedral, a (Catholic) bishop would be required. After twenty minutes, Schuller says, "John and Cheri, you've come to the right place at the right time. These next years will be the most exciting, innovative and dynamic years in the history of this institution. You'll be saying 'Wow!'" This is one of his favorite words; he says it backwards with equal facility. I've never seen anyone so thrilled about a project as he, with such childlike exuberance.

A couple of weeks later, his enthusiasm wanes. The city Building Department rejects his plans. So he starts from scratch, choosing different materials and altering his design. At last completed, dedicated and named in honor of his wife, Arvella, the bells (cast in the Netherlands) transport us to a world of wonder. Baseball's "Angels" are down the street, and Disneyland down another, but here we stand transfixed in an angelic fantasyland. The 1980s and early nineties do, in fact, become the glory days of the Cathedral.

Robert Schuller inaugurated his mega-venture in a drive-in theater in 1955: "Come as you are in the family car". His public persona –bold and visionary – attracts many. After his first buildings are constructed, he provides extensive services for those who are young, old, afflicted, addicted. Strangely, many ascend his fourteen-story "Tower of Hope" only to plunge to their death in suicidal despair. In response, he sets up a twenty-four-hour suicide hotline (an "eye in the sky that never sleeps"). Our good friend Jim Kok, former chaplain at Pine Rest Psychiatric Hospital, Grand Rapids, Michigan, and head of the Cathedral's Pastoral Ministry department, takes charge of this in the 1980s.

Bob tells me that, of the tens of thousands of letters that keep pouring in from TV viewers, the response he receives most frequently is: *"You saved my life!"* – literally. Filled with new hope, they have a reason to live – not because of some theology, but because of the simple and sincere affirmation "You are loved, worthy, and important".

Ironically, in quieter encounters with Bob, I sense some insecurity. Self esteem is the centerpiece of his message to others, but it flows from his own struggles over the years. He proclaims and embodies the ideal image of who he wishes to be. He's an overcomer, a victor, rather than a victim. This drives him. However, in this process of self-improvement, reaching upward and outward, he also tends to overcompensate.

Good thing he has a strong wife to prop him up, and rein him in. Arvella is the real power behind the throne. When he collapses into depressive doldrums, she gives him the courage to keep going. He, in turn, extends that same encouragement to others. Together they have a grand vision; together they implement the details. She takes charge of the *"Hour of Power"* TV production (launched in 1970). Every week she cobbles together the best of three, later two, Sunday morning services. There are many awkward moments, contradictions, incorrect facts that have to be edited. The result is: a seamless, positive, engaging presentation. He's at times rough at the edges; she makes him look good.

With growing demand, Bob decides to set up a seminar for pastors who wish to replicate or emulate his megachurch model. He accommodates. As a result, big box spirituality proliferates everywhere. The key is: *Find a need and fill it.* Ask neighbors what they want, then provide it for them. It's a business model – consumer driven. Problem is: it tends to create authoritarian leaders, especially the right-wing variety. Money and sex scandals have tainted them. Many emphasize power and material success. The 'God and Jesus' stuff for them is masquerade.

What may have started with the best of intentions can gradually go off the rails. And the much-vaunted "Wow!" gets transmogrified into "Ow!"

CHAPTER FORTY.

SELLING A DREAM

Much like Iowa's *"Field of Dreams"* (1989, with Kevin Costner), Iowa-born preacher Robert H. Schuller (1926-2015) is convinced: *"If you build it, they will come"*. He builds a religious tourist attraction, inspired by Disneyland - 'happiest church on earth', where folks can be entertained, inspired and affirmed: 'You are loved, a person of dignity and worth'. It is a place of beauty and grandeur. And so, the Crystal Cathedral opens its doors (1980), as backdrop for the worldwide *"Hour of Power"* television broadcast.

Dr. Frederick Swann, organist of New York's Riverside Church for thirty years, successor to Virgil Fox, is persuaded to defect to the Cathedral (1982-1998), and fills the glass and steel enclosure with sounds sublime and majestic, quieting the spirit, stirring the soul. We're privileged to count him as a friend.

For the next decade, my wife and I entertain Cathedral staff members as guests in our home for Sunday dinner. It gives us clear insight into the inner workings of this mega-enterprise. Unmistakably, the success of this ministry hinges largely on the personality, resourcefulness and integrity of its founder.

An old saying comes to mind: "After all is said and done, there's usually more said than done". In Bob's case, you can be sure, he gets it done!

His achievement is extraordinary. He builds an empire. The question is: Can he keep it?

Schuller is clever. He maximizes viewer contributions to the *"Hour of Power"* by offering 'gifts' as an incentive – like the Dutch "buying" Manhattan from native tribes for a handful of trinkets. He never pays his guests or musical talent, stating: 'We have millions of viewers worldwide. Do yourself a favor: I'm giving you free publicity'. He picks up celebrities on publisher book tours at no cost. Others reward him for an opportunity to appear.

TV viewers want to be entertained and feel relaxed; they love variety, and thirst for good stories. Like Norman Vincent Peale, Schuller is above all a salesman, selling the "American Dream": 'You can be a success. *If you can dream it, you can do it.*' "He tells people exactly what they want to hear in the manner which pleases them most." (Dennis Voskuil, *Mountains Into Goldmines*, 1983) In the process, I should add, he never lets the Bible get in the way of a good message.

One day, I present Bob with a potentially beneficial program for the Cathedral. "John, I'll call my in-house attorney and tell him you're coming right over." I walk two buildings over, and sit down across his desk, when his phone rings. He signals me to stay through the conversation. At the other end of the line are attorneys for the Disney corporation. Disney is in the process of suing the Cathedral. At issue: Schuller had originally hired Disney writers and producers to create *"The Glory of Christmas"*, an impressive (money-making) pageant with actors, organ, choir, instrumentalists, live animals, flying angels – a gripping drama, at least back then.

Bottom line: Schuller shafted them. Disney has the right to receive ongoing royalties. Schuller thought he could circumvent this by having his son-in-law rewrite the script; (the result was a bland remake of the original). The Cathedral is in breach of contract. It's all over the news (not good to have bad press!), and they end up having to pay the piper. That afternoon, I discovered a foundational crack in the house of Schuller, and decided not to pursue my proposal.

Soon thereafter, I discovered another crack. My wife had volunteered to compile and publish a *Crystal Cathedral Choir Cookbook*. Profit: $7,000. It is only one of multiple projects to raise money for a Choir tour of Hawaii. But shortly before the planned departure, the Choir finds its bank account completely wiped out! They are told by Bob's office: a rule exists that, ultimately, the bank accounts of all church organizations are under his personal control, and can be used at his discretion!

It is claimed yet again that he is having trouble meeting payroll that month. But when the books are opened during bankruptcy litigation (2010), it becomes clear these funds had found their way into the pockets of his own family. What had begun as a ministry of self-sacrificial service to others had morphed into nepotism, a cash-cow for the family business – worship of the golden calf, resulting eventually in the fall of the house of Schuller.

In the end, it is Bob's own ego that does him in. He spends a fortune building a monument to himself, a multi-story museum relating the history of his mega-venture, complete with a statue of himself. He dubs it the "Welcome Center". Years before, he had written a book entitled *Being Debt Free*. He boasts that for all the buildings he ever erected, he made sure to have cash on hand for the full amount before proceeding to build.

However, as he gets on in years, concerned about his legacy, he violates his own absolute, cherished principles, visits his friends at Farmer and Merchants Bank, and persuades them to loan him the money! The building is completed; the economy falls on hard times; his TV donation spigot is on low flow; and he suddenly finds himself flat on his face, completely disgraced, having to file for bankruptcy. Because he wants to build a grand monument to himself, like a modern-day Pharaoh, no matter what the cost, he brings defeat on his own head, along with shame and despondency. He loses it all.

In 2012, the Roman Catholic Bishop of the Diocese of Orange in California purchases the bankrupt property, now called Christ Cathedral.

In 2014, Arvella Schuller dies. Bob is found to have cancer, and deteriorates rapidly. Unknown to almost everyone, one of his daughters oversees his placement in the (Reformed) Artesia Christian Home (Artesia, California). She wants his presence kept secret, allowing no visitors. He is barely responsive. Meanwhile, our friend, former staff member at the Cathedral, unaware of Bob's whereabouts, makes regular visits to the Home, providing comfort and encouragement to the elderly.

One day, he gets wind of the big secret. He overhears a nurse mention Bob's name. He follows her, and – sure enough – there he is. From then on, his attitude is: Screw the restrictions! He breaks through the 'No Visitor' blockade and sneaks in whenever he can. He is firmly resolved that, no matter what has transpired in the past: "*I will not let him die alone,* isolated from the world, even from members of his own clan". He holds Bob's hand, while comatose. "You never know what gets through." He reads to him, speaks to him, prays for him. "He's been there for others; now I must be here for him. We all make stupid mistakes; but God loves him, and so do I."

CHAPTER FORTY-ONE.

WHITE EAGLE

C alvin College graduate Feike Feikema (1912-94) is happy to leave behind his restrictive Christian Reformed past in Doon, Iowa. This third-generation Frisian-American, fluent in his ancient tongue, heads for Minneapolis and becomes mayoral candidate Hubert H. Humphrey's assistant campaign manager. But akin to my older brother, he is sidelined in a tuberculosis sanitarium for two years. He has time to reflect; and a deep-seated yearning slowly draws him back to the native soil he later coins *"Siouxland"*.

Feike adopts the pen name Frederick Manfred, and writes the best-seller *Lord Grizzly* (1954), based on the life of American frontiersman Hugh Glass (1783-1833). (*"The Revenant"*, 2015, for which Leonardo di Caprio won a Best Actor Academy Award, is the most recent embellishment of Glass' real-life attack by a grizzly bear in 1823 and his courageous struggle to survive.)

Televangelist Robert H. Schuller (1926-2015) hails from Siouxland. He too gets a taste of the big city, with dreams of super success, but unlike Manfred, decides not to return to the dirt his family farmed. He finds it more convenient to tap into his humble origins rhetorically whenever he can, as a rags-to-riches Horatio Alger story - overcoming poverty, drought, fires and devastating tornadoes.

Bob hears about another prairie boy, from the Rosebud Sioux Indian Reservation, who has left Siouxland for the charms of the city: White Eagle (Mervyn J. Moore, 1951-95). He sang in his preacher-dad's church from age five, and adopted the operatic style of his idol, tenor Mario Lanza. With sterling stage presence and a vibrant voice, Bob offers him guest appearances on the *"Hour of Power"* TV show, and decides to puff him as the greatest tenor since Luciano Pavarotti. Bob exaggerates. (*YouTube: "White Eagle from the Crystal Cathedral"*).

Problem: White Eagle is also an alcoholic. Several times he arrives before the Sunday morning service hammered! He commits to a Twelve-Step program and does his best not to fall off the wagon. At times he does. Sobriety is critical: viewer contributions soar when he's on air, especially from the women-over-fifty demographic.

One day, Schuller receives news that White Eagle is gay and stricken with AIDS. He goes ballistic. For him, alcohol addiction is forgivable, not homosexuality – at least, from a public relations and viewer revenue point of view. His imagined Pavarotti suddenly evaporates - vanishes from the program as if he had never existed, never to be mentioned again! I'm impelled to ask myself: Doesn't this (typically fundamentalist) attitude toward gays negate his essential message of "God loves you" and "Self-Esteem"?

What drives White Eagle to drink? Genes? Influence of the Reservation? Hanging with urban Bohemians? Inner struggle with his closeted sexuality? Perhaps, all of the above.

Several CRC pastors have been defrocked for their gayness! Jack, a highly-gifted seminary classmate, however, simply resigns and becomes a leader of *"Chorus America"* and the Gay Men's Chorus of Washington D.C. – knowing it will take decades for his denomination to come around, if ever.

On November 21, 1987, my wife and I make a special trip to the Episcopal Grace Cathedral on Nob Hill in San Francisco for their inaugural AIDS Memorial Quilt Project. It is a truly moving experience. What is needed is not condemnation, but empathy, understanding and support, change in community attitudes and equitable legislation.

To state the obvious, gays have not fared well through history. They have been imprisoned, tortured, executed. (Hitler slaughtered six million Jewish civilians – horrible enough; but he also extinguished the lives of six million non-Jewish civilians, including gays, gypsies, cults like Jehovah's Witnesses, the mentally ill, terminally ill, severely handicapped persons....)

Oscar Wilde, exposed as gay, was sentenced to two years in prison with hard labor, in late nineteenth-century England, from which he never recovered. English lack of justice also drove outed-Alan Turing (inventor of the Enigma Machine in World War II) to take his own life. British law did not uphold gay rights until 1967. Even so, harassment continued.

In 1969, with the U.S. still lagging behind Great Britain in social legislation, the New York City Police raid Stonewall Inn, a gay bar in Greenwich Village; it provokes an uprising, and the gay liberation movement is born in America.

Mel White (James Melville White) is on the faculty of Fuller Seminary (Pasadena, California) for a decade, and does extensive ghost writing for 'The Evangelical Right' (1960s through 1980s), like a one-man industry – for luminaries including Billy Graham, Jerry Falwell and Pat Robertson. But as soon as he divorces and comes out as gay, they throw him under the bus and condemn him in a most alienating fashion. (See his autobiography *Stranger at the Gate*, 1995, the Forward written by his loving ex-wife.) He marries Gary Nixon at All Saints Episcopal Church, Pasadena, in 2008 – just a block away from Fuller Seminary. Yes, take that! It's legal now. Nevertheless, fundamentalist Christians persist in demonizing the LBGTQ community.

Matthew Shepard, 21-year-old gay university student, is tortured and left for dead, strapped to a barbed wire fence near Laramie, Wyoming in 1998. The reality is horrifying; the symbolism is graphic. *Matthew was crucified for* (on account of) *our sins*. In 2003, the U.S. Supreme Court decriminalized homosexual relations ("The Matthew Shepard Act"). He now lies buried in the National Cathedral, Washington D.C., alongside Helen Keller.

Walking behind a group of conscientious college students last year, busy discussing the problems of the world, one of them said something in contemporary idiom that I think fully applies here. He counsels the group: *"Let's make humanity like a thing again."* Yes, let's!

CHAPTER FORTY-TWO.

SOUND IT OUT

Year 1986

Having read *Why Johnny Can't Read* (1955), by Rudolph Flesch, and *Illiterate America* (1985), by Jonathan Kozol, I waste no time procuring a city business license, an Orange County 'Fictitious Business Name', and State of California incorporation. I sign an office lease agreement, purchase furniture, office supplies, connect phone and utilities, hire the services of an attorney and CPA (bookkeeper/payroll specialist/tax consultant), hire and train a dozen part-time teachers, put up my signage and roll out my advertising. *Whew!*

Why the hurry? 57 percent of Americans are 'functionally illiterate', and wrongly labeled 'dyslexic'. They blame themselves, and try to hide the problem. I can be part of the solution. I'll take the risk; I might go bankrupt trying; if so, so be it. This has to be done.

I take to the airwaves: 'You're not alone. Please call now! I can help.' The response is overwhelming. My teachers work with children and young people – pure phonics: learn to match forty-four sounds with twenty-six letters of the alphabet, plus a handful of simple rules – *Voila!* There's the foundation, followed by spelling and comprehension.

I work with Orange County corporate executives. Too embarrassed to visit my office, I go to them. I say: "You can do this. You were never taught correctly. It's not your fault. Your teachers wanted you to memorize whole words. It's like trying to remember one hundred to one thousand Egyptian hieroglyphs or Chinese characters – an impossible task, whereby reading becomes a guessing game. This may be good for textbook companies; it makes them rich. But many good people are left behind! Let's do *phonics first*. And you'll feel liberated, able to read anything."

Truly amazing! After just a few sessions, they exclaim: "I see it! I can do this." Smothered emotions erupt; tears flow. I'm in the presence of a cathartic miracle. Exit: shame. Enter: self-esteem. *To witness this breakthrough is to experience transcendence.*

For years, these executives have kept the latest issues of the *Wall Street Journal, The Economist, Barron's,* and *Time* magazine prominently displayed on their desk. Their private secretary would read portions to them daily. Now they tackle it on their own. (Yes, I charge a fee. They also prove to be generous.)

Pleased with my results, I become political. Orange County, unfortunately, is dominated by right-wing Republicans. Their Lincoln Club is influential. I disagree with them on everything – except one issue: the need for *'phonics first'* in public education. I storm the offices of a dozen State Senators and Assembly members, making my voice heard. I'm invited to address a policy sub-group of the Party at the Santa Ana Country Club. I also type two single-spaced pages to Republican Governor George Deukmejian (1983-91).

A few lines from that missive: "Illiteracy is a plague on our great Republic. It lowers individual self-esteem, limits educational and occupational choices, and has repercussions for productivity, international competitiveness, and national security. Through private initiative, my company is helping to pick up the pieces where public education has failed. Public schools expect a 35 percent failure rate in the basic skill of reading! They get exactly what they expect. Likewise, we get what we expect: 100 percent reading. Our students' predictable refrain is: 'Why didn't they teach me this back in first grade?' Indeed, why not?"

I conclude: "If 'phonics first' is made mandatory in public education, it will happily make my private business unnecessary." The California Phonics initiative was finally enacted into law one decade later, in 1996.

On my visits to that plethora of politician's offices, the first thing I learn is: many have a nearby facility dedicated to their own re-election. Their campaign is never ending! After all, the perks are great. At one of those offices, an effluvious secretary proudly points to a back room where dirt is processed against political 'enemies'! Hasn't she heard of *"Loose lips sink ships"*? And whatever happened to the commendable tradition of 'honorable adversaries'?

That particular office has it in for Jane Fonda and her husband Tom Hayden, the most liberal and honorable Democratic member of the Assembly. That covert hate-filled cabal works to discredit, defame and destroy - forgetting the old adage: *"By slinging mud you lose ground"*.

President Nixon, via the Departments of Justice and State, had never regarded Fonda's or Hayden's actions, in Vietnam or elsewhere, as illegal or treasonous (though it did infuriate him). It is the Reagan administration, then in power, which hurls these provocative insinuations their way.

Jane Fonda did much to accelerate the end of the Vietnam War. (Ken Burns failed to acknowledge this in his PBS documentary!) She went to North Vietnam with the simple plea that the U.S. stop bombing civilian targets, and stop bombing the dikes – since much of North Vietnam is, like The Netherlands, below sea level. She is a voice for peace, civil rights, economic justice and the environment (*"Standing Rock"*), even going door-to-door to get out the vote in areas of rampant voter suppression. This is altruism at its best.

If literacy can lead to an expanding social consciousness worldwide, let's do it! May the drills of 'sounding it out' serve to empower the poor and disenfranchised as equal partners in the pursuit of freedom, truth, justice and peace.

CHAPTER FORTY-THREE.

A HIGHER CALLING

Year 1988

I open another business – in Los Angeles County, focused on the prosperous Palos Verdes Peninsula, increasingly populated by people of Asian extraction, then affectionately known by some as "Rice Hill".

Dutch-born, I am genetically a middle man. But where can I find a niche? Roofing. Are you kidding? There's already an oversupply of roofers! True, but I see top-quality mom-and-pops struggling, while the big guys gobble up most of the customers. I will broker for the little guy. I market; they install. I can outsell anybody.

I'll advertise, climb on roofs, measure and diagram, do estimates, write contracts, divvy up the work to selected installers, and ensure customer satisfaction. I know my contractors' costs; I'll do a simple retail markup.

So I market proven quality at a fair price. It's lucrative. I've never before earned so much money. During these one dozen years of brokering contracts, I sit down with hundreds of couples at their kitchen table. If you make it to the table, you're half way to a signed contract. Very few people in large cities allow strangers into their home. It's good to be invited in.

The biggest problem with in-home sales is not the blaring TV, which I politely ask them to turn off, nor a phone ringing, which I ask them to silence, but the obstacle at the front door – the dog that greets you, sniffing your crotch! Embarrassing. Annoying. Subconsciously voyeuristic, paranoid, or sadistic customers seem to enjoy this vicarious spectacle of humiliation. If you pass the sniff test, and manage not to get castrated, you may enter.

Traditionally, Calvinists believe that all legitimate callings are of equal honor. But I keep getting the question: What's a preacher doing fiddling on a roof? I reply: "I'm getting up in the world"; "I'm a little closer to heaven". My favorite: *"I've found a higher calling"*.

I discover that selling something, or providing a service, is not really what interests me. It's people. I can't let go of my pastoral instincts. So I listen. People, somehow, feel comfortable sharing their life story, their troubles, fears, and all. I'm not a therapist, nor do I wish to be. Many feel isolated and need a friend. Others have kept things bottled up so long, they can no longer contain themselves, and let it all out. It's therapeutic.

Time flies by. *Something magical happens* – as if a higher power in the room forges a momentary spiritual bond. At a critical point, however, my internal clock sends me an alert, and I exclaim: "Wow, I almost forgot why I came here! When shall we get started on your roof?" Without actually selling, I am nevertheless flooded with contracts. This is not some clever technique; that would be cynical and degenerate.

I do not follow the prevailing prescriptions of sales gurus; I follow my experience and conscience. Material rewards, as they come, I regard as pure gifts, which must be paid forward. The kitchen table closings are as great an adventure in pastoral psychology as I had ever experienced in my churches. The world has become my parish.

Several of my clients are Japanese-Americans. One in particular comes to mind, a gentleman whose family – following the attack on Pearl Harbor, December 7, 1941 – is forced out of their home by agents of the federal government and transported to the hastily-constructed Manzanar Internment Camp (California Highway 395, east side of the Sierras, south of Bishop). It is only one of dozens of Camps throughout the U.S. which unjustly detain citizens during World War II.

Ito's family has lost everything. The home and business they've been forced to abandon are placed in the hands of non-Japanese-American "caretakers" for "safekeeping". Soon they are betrayed. Their properties and possessions are sold out from under them! Robbed blind, disenfranchised, utterly humiliated, they sit and wait, hoping that someday they'll regain freedom on the outside, able to make a new start.

Ito's family faces indefinite detention, without cause or due process, based on a nation's irrational fears and certain opportunists' criminal intent. Perhaps these prisons are not exact copies of Hitler's concentration camps, or of Stalin's Gulag; yet, they're deplorable – surrounded by fences, barbed wire, watch towers, armed guards and attack dogs. Really?! They're a threat? This is by no means FDR's finest hour!

Ito's family lost everything; but they still have each other. Moreover, they can use their skills for the benefit of the whole – cooking, sewing, storytelling, tutoring, entertaining, exercising, cleaning. As long as they cooperate, they are not coerced; neither do they wish to remain idle.

Ito is a hormonal teenager. He and his buddies know how to have fun. There are sports, games and classes on site; there are also girls. So, he recounts, they'd crawl into the attics of the longhouse barracks. They know precisely where every family is housed, and where the peek holes are (which they themselves created!). Having no Sears-Roebuck catalogues available for their erotic pleasure, what's a young robust male to do?

One day, they are caught. A scantily-dressed girl hears a noise above her ceiling, suspects who's up there, and turns them in. Life in the Camp! So, the boys are given a choice: select one of three punishments; or else, serve Uncle Sam as translators in the Pacific Theater of the War. They choose the latter. Wise choice.

This way, they're able to escape the Camp, experience a new structured freedom, demonstrate their loyalty to the nation, learn new skills, enjoy post-war opportunities for higher education (GI Bill), Veteran's benefits, and make an entirely new life for themselves.

After the War, Ito launches a profitable nursery and landscaping business, benefiting his entire extended family. He encourages others: '*Never give up. Let's pool our resources and work our way back to the top.*'

Back to the top they came. Though it took forever before the U.S. compensated them for their losses - too little, too late (only pennies on the dollar), a new governing generation did thereby acknowledge an earlier generation's guilt. No doubt, there are chapters in our history some would rather forget. We must never forget.

CHAPTER FORTY-FOUR.

ROYAL SMILDE

My birthplace of Heerenveen produced Wim Duisenberg (1935-2005), first President of the European Central Bank (1998-2003), the Alan Greenspan of Europe, who midwifed the Euro. It also gave birth to Olympic speed-skating champion Sved Kramer (1986). The list is long. Setske de Haan (1889-1948), pen name Cissy van Marxveldt, the Louisa May Alcott of the Netherlands, drew her first breath in Oranjewoud, the enchanted woods on the edge of town. Anne Frank read her novels and chose to emulate her style.

Another notable was born in 1926, whose business savvy became legendary. His great grandfather established a slaughterhouse in 1863, which by 1900 began rendering animal fats into tallow and lard, a *sine qua non* for the Western palate. Assuming the reins of the family business in 1960, and energized by the U.S. *"Marshall Plan"*, Dirk expands their enterprise into a vast food conglomerate, with twenty-four factories throughout Europe, and dozens of familiar labels on supermarket shelves. On its 125th anniversary (1988), the family crown jewel is honored with the title *"Koninklijke"* – Royal Smilde.

Dirk purchases an estate in Oranjewoud, the forest made famous in the seventeenth century, the "Golden Age" of Dutch conquest and culture, by its Royal Palace. The Smilde estate, *"Klein Jagtlust"* (built 1857), is in the National Registry of Historic Places, with 12½ acres of formal gardens, trees and ponds. He adds a greenhouse, vegetable garden, aviary, pool and tennis court. All in all, a taste of heaven.

Entering the grounds of *"Klein Jagtlust"* in 1989 gives me the feeling I am back in the *"Vijverhof"* paradise of my youth. I tug at the doorbell of the manor house. Dirk answers. "You're little Jan, Simon's boy? Yes...yes, I remember! You used to peddle your little bike all over town and stop for treats at our factory. Come in, come in! We have more treats for you." I am warmly embraced and made to feel like family. Another 'Gump moment' - leading to a special friendship, regular correspondence and frequent visits spanning over two decades.

Long before Smilde becomes *"Royal"*, my father is its bookkeeper (1920-50), accountant, office manager, and in times of crisis (Great Depression, World War II), purchasing and sales agent on the road in the company's black Ford. His allotment of lard, with its high barter value, saves us in the War years. He is scrupulous, honest, self-sacrificing - character traits shared by Dirk.

After five years of bloody war, Germany surrenders in 1945. Resistance leaders find themselves in the role of town administrators for two years, until elections are held. Dad is put in charge of the *"Crackstate"* prison-annex, which under German command had been one of the cruelest torture chambers in the land. Now it houses defeated Nazis and Dutch traitor-collaborators.

Can you imagine having to feed those who betrayed and slaughtered your close relatives, friends and neighbors? At first, he spits in the food he serves them. Gradually, he sees the wisdom of rehabilitation alongside punishment. War brings out the best and the worst in us. Our instincts may dictate cruel retribution, but will that ever end the cycle of vengeance?

At war's end, Dad helps orient Dirk to the nuts and bolts of the business, grooming him for his future role as company CEO. His friendship with my parents later finds my wife and me riding the coattails of Dirk's success, beneficiaries of his largesse. At our biennial stayovers, Dirk chauffeurs us in his beloved Bentley to fascinating places and events. Best seats in the house, always. At a performance of Bach's *"St. Matthew Passion"*, Pieterskerk in Leiden, we notice Princess Christina seated directly in front of us!

Dirk erects a new church building, donating it to his congregation. He installs a pipe organ, but with the proviso that he be principal organist until his demise. (Not too much to ask. Luckily, he plays well.) He establishes fellowships in his name at the University of Groningen, sponsors medical relief work in Africa, and major Dutch sporting events (skating, sailing, cycling, soccer). To enhance his (traditional) congregation's library, I send him the two hundred volumes of Dutch biblical studies, commentaries and theology I had been given in 1966 by the Stated Clerk of the CRC, who had particular hopes for me which I did not appropriate as my own. My interests took a more progressive turn.

Our monthly correspondence over twenty-four years, written long-hand and mailed, centers on business, world affairs, religion and American history, including 'New Netherland'. We discuss new publications at length (for example, Simon Shama, *The Embarrassment of Riches: An Interpretation of Dutch Culture in the Golden Age*, 1988; Russell Shorto, *The Island at the Center of the World*, 2005). Religious studies stir both fascination and vigorous debate (for instance, my conservative nephew-in-law Anthony J. Tomasino's *Judaism Before Jesus*, 2003, and my more progressive cousin-in-law Daniel L. Pals' *Seven Theories of Religion*, 1996, later expanded to nine theories, and still considered a standard work in university departments of religion).

Dirk knows of my ties with progressive theologians. That doesn't faze him. He's strong in his own convictions, doesn't feel threatened, and treats me as an equal. He's one of the most tolerant people of conservative persuasion I have known. If only his temperament were more universal!

A few months after Royal Smilde celebrates its 150th anniversary in 2013, Dirk dies. The empire he built remains a family legacy. Good continues to flow from it.

CHAPTER FORTY-FIVE.

PARADOX

Year 2017

My barber of the last thirty-some years decides to retire: "John, it's been a good run, but everybody's got an expiration date, and mine's right around the corner. I'm decelerating."

"Come on, Bob you're not over the hill yet!"

"No, but I'd rather be over it than under it!"

Bob's a clever *"Popular Science"* kind of guy. There's endless repartee between him and the chair. He adds a metaphor: "Time races on, and the snowball rolls faster and faster downhill."

"Wow, sounds like acceleration. But Bob, first you said you were slowing down; now things are speeding up. Which is it? Acceleration or deceleration?"

"It's a paradox. My slowing down is speeding up."

"Your snowball rolling downhill, however, gets bigger and bigger, not smaller."

"Yes, it gets bigger because it rolls faster with every revolution. Gravity. But the way I picture it: there's a monumental implosion at the end of the roll, like one of Einstein's black holes."

"You mean like Mot, the Canaanite god of Death – literally, the "Swallower" – which is why Paul punned "Mot will be swallowed up in victory."

"John, you're theology; I'm science."

"No, I have my ear to both. Einstein drew on imagery from many sources, while working out his ingenious equations. Science makes strides ahead through imagination."

Bob waxes academic: "I visualize implosion as analogous to our end of life, because it returns us to the basic state of our composite elements which, according to the laws of energy, can neither be created nor destroyed. *Voila!* Eternal life, that is, Existence."

"You're right, can't argue with the Second Law of Thermodynamics. Analogies, unfortunately, do tend to melt down at a certain point. It's *your offspring* that gets bigger, not smaller. Ancient Greeks believed 'Eternal Life' came in two forms: Offspring and Fame. The former proved to be more enduring than the latter."

I say farewell, as my barber is about to step out for lunch. "I wish you all the happiness in the world, and many good *repostes*!"

"You didn't say 'Repose', did you?"

"Not yet!"

I have further need of someone versed in the tonsorial arts, so I step inside the shop of a recent Guatemalan immigrant. After a lifetime of barbers, I now move up in the world: I have a hairdresser. She's funny, vivacious, attentive. She seats me in a chair next to the door, which always remains open. (Come one, come all.)

Well, come she did – a woman in her sixties, walking stick in hand – right up to my chair: "What beautiful hair you have! You look just like my next door neighbor; he's Dutch. Are you athletic, like me? How old are you?" On and on! I assumed everybody knew her. They didn't. This gal is plumb loco - reminding me of a visit to that psychiatric hospital in Chicago.

An open-door policy may be advantageous, but if any derelict can drift in…. I'd better put an end to this: "Thank you, dear, for your generous compliments. I'll be sure to share this with my wife." My, did she ever hightail it out of there!

My hairdresser grinned: "There are a lot of widows out there, Juanito. You don't wear a ring, do you? That'll get you into trouble every time."

"Sure about that?"

"I know; I watch soap operas."

With such sage advice, I determine that henceforth she, a comely purveyor of charm, will become my beautician.

CHAPTER FORTY-SIX.

SHY OF EXUBERANT

Today is my birthday, the fourth dreary day of sitting, waiting in a jury pool room of the California Superior Court. I feel like Dr. Lewis Smedes when, years back, as I heard tell, he stood before the Synod of the Christian Reformed Church in Grand Rapids and was asked: *"What is hell?"* Having already endured hours of rigorous and contentious examination, he blurted out: "It's like flying in a holding pattern over O'Hare for four hours!" That's not the answer they were looking for. Needless to say, the old denominational stalwarts were not amused, and passed him over as Chair of Ethics, Calvin Seminary. You're right, Smedes. That's hell!

Mid-afternoon, my name is drawn. My mind tries putting a positive spin on it: just think of it as another day of fishing, except this time it's fishing for truth.

The defense attorney, in the jury selection process, asks me: "Do you tend to be on the side of law enforcement?"

I reply, "Yes, I do – unless it can be shown that officers have violated our communal trust." I add, "Unfortunately, some have gone off the reservation – which in ancient Greece, prompted philosophers to ask *'But who will guard the Guardians?'*"

He seems quite unsure whether to accept or dismiss me, and presses on, "Well, how do you feel about serving on a jury?"

I answer, *"Just shy of exuberant!"* - which even draws a hearty laugh from the poker-faced Judge.

"Okay, can you be impartial and objective in a case where an older black woman, whether in self-defense or not, is accused of assault on her husband with a deadly weapon?"

I pause, and retort, "Gender and age are totally irrelevant."

I can't believe it. Defense Counsel stares me down for one full minute (it seems longer), without saying a word. I lock eyes with him, not blinking, in this duel of wits with a hungry predator. It's what I didn't say that has him in a quandary. No, I'm as far from racist as East is from West, but let him infer what he wishes. Others would have seen through me and had me impaneled on this jury. The Attorney thankfully does not, and asks for my dismissal.

I love courtroom drama! Luckily, this drama resulted in a happier birthday.

CHAPTER FORTY-SEVEN.

DASHING IN BLACK

December 2017

Br-r-r! While many survive a deep freeze in Michigan, we bask in California sunshine, watching (Grand Rapids' Chris Van Allsburg's) *Polar Express (2004)*. Before our eyes we see a famous old landmark – Herpolsheimer's, with its superb animated Christmas window displays. Happy memories.

Politically, things are not so happy. Women are still trampled on. Hoorah for the Women's March (January 2017), the Me Too Movement and the recent *USA Today* editorial (December 13, 2017), which states: "A president who would all but call Senator Kirsten Gillibrand a whore is not fit to clean the toilets of Barack Obama's Presidential Library...."

Add to this the book by 27 leading psychiatrists, *The Dangerous Case of Donald Trump* (October, 2017). Sum: the guy's a sociopath – angry, volatile, unstable – an extreme danger here-and-now. And just out, yet another corroborative bombshell: Michael Wolff's *Fire and Fury: Inside the Trump White House* (2017).

My own impressions to date (with apologies for my opprobrious and vulgar language): Who is this malodorous miscreant forever taxing our tolerance, who *speaks words without knowledge (Job 38:2)*, whose *trump gives an uncertain sound (I Cor. 14:8)*, who sows confusion, incites violence, pisses on women and tweets out of his ass! Exemplary leader?

On the contrary, he lies, cheats, steals; he's a racist, narcissist, criminal, bully, con-artist, swamp creature, antichrist, destroyer of democracy...*ad infinitum*. He is, in my opinion, "*The Chaos President*"! Fitting epitaph: "*The Ultimate Loser*", his own worst enemy. "The fish rots from the head down," Ronald Reagan used to say.

Steven Spielberg's film *The Post* (2017) is timely – drawing parallels between the Nixon and Trump presidencies. Its subject, Daniel Ellsberg, is a true American hero, making the Pentagon Papers accessible to the American people, with the aid of courageous publishers. He thereby accelerated the end to a war we never should have fought, and the end of a demagogue in high office.

A real surprise is Ellsberg's new book, *The Doomsday Machine: Confessions of a Nuclear War Planner* (2017). Who knew that since the late 1950s he was also an elite nuclear strategist for the RAND Corporation – one of the 'Whiz Kids' – and a special assistant to Secretary of Defense Robert McNamara. Ellsberg eventually came to see the utter futility of the nuclear option - as a zero-sum game. His warnings are most timely in the current standoff with North Korea.

What a year - *2017*! Consider the drama at the United Nations War Tribunal in The Netherlands, when imprisoned General Slobodan Praljak becomes the seventeenth of his compatriots to be convicted of war crimes (crimes against humanity: ethnic cleansing, genocide). To the bitter end he exhibits raw hatred for Bosnian Muslims. His former life as a theater director must have inspired his inflated ego to exclaim, with heightened drama: "I am not a war criminal!" (Sure – like Nixon? "I am not a crook!") – whereupon, he throws back his head and drinks a vial of cyanide *(fast-acting, 'ask your doctor....')* It strikes me that, since he had also been a professor of philosophy, he is trying to be a Socrates (ordered by the State to end his life, drinking the hemlock). But Praljak, you're no Socrates! (Like Lloyd Bentsen in the 1988 televised vice-presidential debate with Senator Dan Quayle: "Senator, you're no Jack Kennedy!") Praljak was found guilty, yet remained Trump-like defiant to the end. Clearly, he is no martyr; he is the ultimate coward! He takes no responsibility for his unconscionable actions. He will not be missed by civilized humanity.

Ethnic cleansing has likewise blemished Burma. Burmese military generals (goons) and Buddhist mobs are slaughtering and expelling Rohingya Muslims! Almost a million refugees have crossed the border into Bangladesh. Prime Minister Aung San Suu Kyi should have her Nobel Peace Prize revoked for acquiescing in this genocide.

I admit, the preceding has been a little heavy, but it's the world in which we live.

On a lighter note: I can't believe my eyes! Suddenly, in the swimming pool lane next to mine, a dashing figure in black appears - a vigorous competitor, grace incarnate, eyes on the mark, seemingly effortless strong steady strokes – dressed from head to toe in a *hijab*, only her determined face visible.

Instantly I recall the Junior Lifeguard class at Fuller Park, July 1957. We are required to jump into the pool fully clothed to rescue a 'drowning' person. Waterlogged clothes are like a lead vest. So, I have all the more admiration for the fully-clothed Muslim swimming alongside me – faster than me, indomitable, made of steel. I don't know her story. One can only speculate. She disappears after fifteen minutes. I imagine her as someone pushing back at the restraints of custom, not wanting to be anyone's chattel, but on her way to liberation. After all, this is the USA; and perhaps, in this open, liberal society her metamorphosis will take place, and a butterfly will emerge from the Chrysalis. Who knows?

Our Muslim swimmer reminds me of Martin Luther's wife. Luther was at his swashbuckling best helping young women escape forced intern-ment in nunneries, placing one Katarina von Bora in a barrel. He sneaks her out of the convent in the dead of night, then eventually marries her in Wittenberg, at a time when ex-priests and ex-nuns are wed by the hundreds. (*Celibacy is not hereditary.* It's a choice, not to be imposed by debauched popes.) Katarina emerged from the Chrysalis as a liberated, elegant butterfly, and the Protestant Reformation was launched anew.

It's good to be in the tradition of Protest and Reform.

CHAPTER FORTY-EIGHT.

TRUE MEASURE

To feel the warmth of the sun is to experience the miraculous. It is another perfect day on Lake Mojave – not fishing today, but piloting the rented aluminum craft, with its fifteen-horsepower outboard motor twenty miles north, from Katherine Landing to Cottonwood Cove.

On our return, halfway back, in the middle of this vast body of water, still far from shore, the unexpected happens – we're enveloped in clouds, menaced by turbulent winds, riding tumultuous swells – internally screaming *'Help! We'll be swamped!'* My wife keeps bailing out water; I slow the motor, zigzagging over the waves.

This is not a motion picture studio's tempest in a bathtub; it's the real thing, with genuine bowel-busting fear! We struggle with nature for endless hours. We're not in the safe embrace of some invincible ocean liner, nor in the tranquil depths with protective gear and oxygen tanks like George Bass and Robert Ballard. We're blind in the middle of nowhere – no navigation tools, no stabilizer. It's our Galilean Lake, but nobody walking on the water saying "Peace, be still!"

Wonder of wonders, we're back at the landing by nightfall. Puttering up to the dock, the attendants express their amazement: "You just survived a Red Flag emergency!"

"It's great to be alive!"

We collapsed into bed, and rode out the storm once more.

Sunshine is a miracle; cessation of turmoil is a miracle; life is a miracle.

Shortly thereafter, my wife and I check into the Rio Hotel, Las Vegas for a couple of nights – home of magicians Penn and Teller, and the glamorous well-sculpted Chippendale men. Taking the elevator up to our suite, three young men in their twenties bounce in (all a little chubby). I think I'll have a little fun with them: "Are you those Chippendale guys?" Laughter. Two of them look embarrassed, but the third fellow perks up. He glows; he's enchanted; that's his dream - though his body hasn't quite caught up. As they step out, I chirp, "We're really looking forward to your show tonight!" More laughter.

Would you believe, a few hours later, as we enter the elevator, that beaming young man comes on board. I say, "Hi! I'm sorry we had to miss your performance tonight. It must have been fabulous!" Under his breath he mumbles *"If only...."* I leave him with a few words he will most surely remember, as he steps out: "Well, keep in mind – *there are many different ways of taking the true measure of a man."* He looks bemused. Something to think about.

CHAPTER FORTY-NINE.

DEEP SPACE

August 25, 2017. *Air Canada, LAX to Montreal*

It's Montreal's 375th birthday, and Canada's 150th. We're on our way to help celebrate - and sure enough, another frequently rare *'Gump moment'* materializes.

An educated professional with youthful vitality takes the aisle seat next to me. He chats with colleagues nearby and appears to be their inspiration. He's polite to me, but somewhat guarded. *CIA?*

His English is impeccable; yet he's reading the French translation of a Bill Bryson book. *He must be Quebecois.* So I ask: "Is Montreal your hometown?" Yes. He mentions he's returning from a NASA meeting at JPL (Jet Propulsion Laboratory, Pasadena). *Scientist?*

To open a door to further dialogue, I remark: "That's interesting. I've been a member of the Skeptics Society the last dozen years (Michael Shermer, founder). We meet at Caltech (California Institute of Technology). It's always attended by a good number of JPL personnel."

"But you have a religious background."

"That's true, but I believe religion should be closely scrutinized by scientific disciplines. I'm not like the proverbial cleric who said: 'A long career as a preacher has fully equipped me to speak with great authority on vast subjects about which I know precious little.'" He chuckles, and I add: "Skepticism is critical thinking, a scientific attitude and method to ascertain truth; *but I reject it as a worldview or way of life.*"

That little tidbit of personal information opens the floodgates. He formally introduces himself: "Oh, by the way, I'm Sylvain Laporte, President of the Canadian Space Agency." Now he feels free to speak and share his opinions.

After watching an episode of *"Guardians of the Galaxy"*, he stands up, looks out our window, and points excitedly: "John, look down there! It's Utah – NASA's Mars simulation site (a landscape similar to Mars). Several of my people are down there right now checking out the latest rover robotics and controls.... I and the rest of my team are headed back to headquarters in Longueuil (suburb of Montreal)."

I can't believe it! In 1970, it was Robert Ballard, the about-to-become world-famous Deep Sea archeologist of *Titanic* fame; now, I'm in dialogue with a champion of Deep Space – a leader and policy-maker. I remark: "It must be exciting being right at the edge of tomorrow. You create new opportunities for research, commercial development, military defense, as well as planetary exploration...."

"Yes, it's exciting. I just wish we had more funds available for cutting-edge projects (also a common NASA lament). Notice that my colleagues and I are flying coach, not first class. We all have to do our part."

"For my part, I'm glad you're flying coach." Whereupon, I tell him how impressed I was five years ago with the spectacular landing on Mars of the Curiosity rover, using a skycrane landing system developed by the rocking-rolling Adam Seltzner, instant media celebrity, and now JPL Chief Engineer of the Mars 2020 Project.

"Yes, that's precisely why we're here – cooperating on this Project, to help lay the groundwork for sending humans to Mars in the 2030s." He then recounts Canada's history in space, in league with NASA – the 1962 launch of its first satellite from Vandenberg Air Force Base, nine astronauts, and a space sector that now employs ten thousand people (supporting twenty-five thousand jobs in the national economy).

I ask him about Canadian satellites in orbit. Surveillance? Spying? No answer. Weather related? Yes, extremely important: ozone, global warming, rising oceans. The menace of 'space junk'? He's concerned. "But how can the clutter be contained when a French start-up company called 'One Web Satellites' has 300 full-time engineers working to send up 900 commercial satellites by the end of 2019? I just read about this." It's a challenge.

"And what do you think about 'space tourism'?" He thinks it's obscene. "Well," I continue, "one day, before I die, I wish to take a regularly-scheduled commercial suborbital flight from Los Angeles to Sydney, Australia in 39 minutes flat, 'up, down, and there you are!'" This sounds more agreeable to him.

Laporte is suddenly animated. He talks about *the Cassini orbiter* which has been up for twenty years, has penetrated several rings of Saturn and visited its moons – scheduled to self-destruct in three weeks, September 14, as it hurtles closer to the planet. Breathtaking breakthroughs! Then, it was on to Black Holes and the Kuiper Belt – a little out of my orbit!

Before we part ways, I ask Mr. Laporte what excites him more than anything else about the exploration of space. His inner child surfaces as he recounts: "I loved science fiction since I was a kid. I dreamed of visiting distant planets, meeting human counterparts. My passion today is exoplanets – planets outside our solar system, both within our Milky Way galaxy, and beyond. What drives me is the quest for life and sentient beings out there, while our search tools are improving every day." Carl Sagan's *Cosmos* (1980s), it appears, has had a salubrious effect on our Mr. Laporte.

"So, are there a dozen or more planets like ours out there capable of sustaining life as we know it?"

"A dozen? The mathematical probability is at least thousands or tens of thousands! Based on 2013 Kepler space mission data, current estimates suggest that, on the low side, there are forty billion earth-size planets orbiting habitable zones of stars like our sun. The mathematical likelihood? Extremely high. The only problem is, of course, they're so far away. We may come to know a lot about some of them, but it may be physically impossible to encounter them."

He introduces me to his second in command, and we exit the plane.

Sufficient stimulation for one flight!

I remain in awe of the marvels of modern science, and glory in its beneficent use.

Ad astra – to the stars!

POSTSCRIPT

Year 2020

Looks as if the devastating Coronavirus pandemic may linger longer; we're still sequestered. I confess to my wife: "Honey, bless me for I have sinned. It has been six months since my last haircut; I look like an old hippie, and I'm ten pounds overweight!"

"Bless you, my beloved Neanderthal. Hie thee unto yon salon, and no more ice cream! *Pax vobiscum.*"

"Am I absolved?"

"Only if you hug me, you shaggy dog. We're in this thing together."

BIBLIOGRAPHY

De Vries, Peter. *The Blood of the Lamb*. New York: Little, Brown & Company, 1961.

Didion, Joan. *Salvador*. New York: Simon and Schuster, 1983.

_____. *Slouching Towards Bethlehem*. New York: The Noonday Press, 1968.

_____. *The White Album*. New York: Simon and Schuster, 1979.

Littlefair, Duncan E. *The Glory Within You: Modern Man and the Spirit*. Philadelphia: The Westminster Press, 1973.

Scheeres, Julia. *Jesus Land*. New York: Counterpoint, 2005.

Swieringa, Robert P., "Masselink Challenges the Cicero Mob," *Origins* 24, no. 1 (2006): 36-41.

Van Til, Reinder, and Gordon Olson, eds. *Thin Ice: Coming of Age in Grand Rapids*. Grand Rapids: Eerdmans, 2007.

ABOUT THE AUTHOR

*Tuna Fisch is the pen name of John Kommerinus Tuinstra,
former pastor, educator and entrepreneur.
He lives with his wife Dr. Cheri Tuinstra
in San Diego, California.*

INDEX OF NAMES